From Victim

to Victor

Turning Tragedy Into Triumph

Fairmont

BOOKS

by

Roger DeFoe

rogerdefoe@netzero.net

Fairmont Books is a ministry of The McDougal Foundation, Inc., a Maryland nonprofit corporation dedicated to spreading the Gospel of the Lord Jesus Christ to as many people as possible in the shortest time possible.

Published by:

Fairmont Books

P.O. Box 3595
Hagerstown, MD 21742-3595
www.mcdougal.org

ISBN 1-58158-009-6

Printed in the United States of America
For Worldwide Distribution

Come to Me, all you who labor and are heavy laden, and I will give you rest. Take My yoke upon you and learn from Me, for I am gentle and lowly in heart, and you will find rest for your souls.

Jesus, NKJ

Dedication

To my father, RALPH: You demonstrated to us the real meaning of manhood. Your priorities were in order and your needs simple. Words came hard for you, but your life spoke volumes. Even when you were in your seventies, I still walked proud and tall next to you. Thank you for your sacrificial giving and your friendship. I will never forget you.

To my mother, MARY: All my life I watched with amazement and great pleasure at the way you cared for us. From homemade bread to handsewn clothing, you gave us treasures beyond imagination. Many were the times I challenged your love, and you always met that challenge with the utmost dignity and class. I think I have never met anyone with greater love, one who looked beyond the frailty of human flesh and dared to be vulnerable. You were the greatest.

To my sister CAROL: If ever a friend there was, it was you. You have been my sounding board and a true inspiration for me. The gentleness and love that are so deeply ingrained in you are qualities that seem to have escaped me all too often. I count on you for guidance, and I cherish your acceptance when I am less than I should be. If I could choose a sister, it would be you.

To my daughter BECCA: At just four years of age, you taught me more about life than I had known in thirty-four years. You faced death with a courage I had never found and am yet searching for. Your charming smile and contagious laughter will forever be with me. Whenever I am inclined to surrender to life's pain and its pressures, I remember … and I stand again. *"Thanks be unto God for His unspeakable gift."*

To my pastor, TIM BAGWELL: You may never know how much you have impacted my life. In a time when I trusted no one, I learned to trust you with the issues of my soul. Though some find you harsh, I see the great love that commands the words to flow from within your spirit. It is that loving encouragement that has kept me on track when I have felt like giving up. Like a river that quenches a thirsty soul, you feed us so well each week. Your prayers watch over us; your words guide us toward *"the mark of the prize."* I love you, pastor.

To my friend BOB: Words fail me to describe what is in my heart concerning you. Perhaps you are God's surgeon, gently performing the skillful work that must be done in order to transform me into His handiwork, or the beacon that steadily points toward the safe landing of His plan for my life. We are two hearts uniting in a common purpose — to see the work He began in them to be completed. For the many hours you have graciously given, both in prayer and in person, I am forever grateful, and I am proud to call you friend.

To my friend ARLENE: You came to us with a pillow in one hand and a "rod" in the other, determined to rid us of the demons that had perplexed our souls and kept us in the dark regions of life. Without you, I recognize that this book would either not have been written or, at the very least, would have been delayed until our Father had chosen another way to set me free and get me on my way home. More than a counselor or friend, you have been a soulmate, in a sense. We are fellow travelers, you and I, and as such we are able to build one another up. I treasure your support in my darkest hours, and *"I thank God upon every remembrance of you."*

Contents

Foreword by Dr. Tim Bagwell

Senior Pastor, Word of Life Christian Center

I met Roger DeFoe in 1993 when he began attending Word of Life Christian Center in Littleton, Colorado. Through the years we have built a strong relationship, and I'm proud to say I have seen him set free from the mindset of a victim and watched him becoming a victor. As you read this book, I believe the Holy Spirit will take you on a journey and, hopefully, by revelation, you will understand that you, too, can leave the places of bondage and wandering and press into a place of God-given promise. Roger empties his heart in this book with one major mission: that through the heartaches of his life and the revelation that brought breakthroughs, he will be able to help you to become the conqueror that Christ has ordained you to be.

Introduction by Bob Murphy

Like Jacob in the Old Testament, we all walk with a limp from encounters in our past, our burdens weigh us down, and life seemingly overwhelms us. At times, we tend to forget who we *now are* and focus on who and what we *used to be.* The good news (the Gospel) is that our Lord Jesus Christ rescued us from our circumstances and in Him we are *"a new creation"* (2 Corinthians 5:17).

The enemy wants to keep us living in our past, and all too often we willingly oblige him. As difficult as it is to admit it, we choose to remain victims instead of believing in and acting on the promises and provisions of Christ Jesus.

First, we need a revelation of those promises.

Only a few years ago, Roger could not have written this book because he was all too willing to see himself as a victim of his past. Life had "dealt" him several personal tragedies, and in his pain and grief Roger had taken on the mantle of victim.

It was during one of his times of trial that our pastor approached me and said, "Keep an eye on Roger. Don't let him slip through the cracks." That request was confirmation of a message the Holy Spirit had placed in my spirit days earlier. Roger was my friend, and he was hurting. I needed to be there for him and walk with him in his journey through the valley. In the days ahead, I needed to help him maintain his focus on the One who was able (and willing) to deliver him from the pain and anguish of his circumstances.

Many times over the next several months, Roger would share his hurts with me, and together we would seek God. Our goal was not to become mired in self-pity, but to consider *what would Jesus do?* in every circumstance. When people would heap guilt on Roger, we would try to understand what Jesus would do in that circumstance. When Roger would be attacked from an unexpected source, we would consider *what would Jesus do?* Thankfully, throughout it all, Roger consistently refused to assume the role of victim and instead chose to be a victor.

Roger has often told his adult daughter, "I cannot speak to you from my successes, but I will speak from my failures." Our "failures," however, are *not* failures if we grow from them and use these experiences to help and encourage others to grow. This book is but one example of how Roger has done just that.

This is not a book about failures, and it's not about Roger. It is a testimony to the healing power of God. From the first teaching chapter, "Egypt: The Making of a Victim," through the final one, "Peter: The Ultimate Victor," Roger takes the reader through the steps outlined in the Word of God for attaining victory.

If you feel that you're a victim, choose today to be a victor. If someone close to you is burdened with the mantle of a victim, come alongside that person and help him to see that God has ordained him to be a victor.

As you read this book, let the Holy Spirit speak to you and reveal God's plan for your life, always remembering:

> *Yet in all these things we are more than conquerors through Him who loved us.*
> Romans 8:37 (NKJ)

We overcome by the blood of the Lamb, and we are victors.

My life has been blessed because God chose me to walk with Roger during a difficult time in his life, and I thank Him for that privilege.

Part I

From Victim to Victor

Now unto Him that is able to do exceeding abundantly above all that we ask or think, according to the power that worketh in us, unto Him be glory in the church by Christ Jesus throughout all ages, world without end. Amen.

Paul

Chapter 1

A Modern-Day Job

It was a little before 2:00 A.M. when we finally said good-bye to our daughter Becca. The past ten months had taken their toll on all of us, but the last few days had been by far the most difficult. After she had been diagnosed with AUL, a rare and deadly form of leukemia, Becca had fought it bravely. It was painful to watch her suffer so intensely now. Near the end, we were told that she was receiving enough morphine to kill a horse. Still, she screamed in pain.

Next to her, Becca's mother and I sat uneasily, neither of us speaking to the other. We were separated, and although we managed to temporarily set aside our hostilities for Becca's sake, the peace was a tense one at best.

Finally, Becca took her last breath, and mercifully

she was gone. Each of us spent a some time alone with her, and then I left to get some rest.

My rest proved to be short-lived. I was awakened by a phone call informing me that I needed to make funeral arrangements immediately because Becca's insurance was in my name. It was Friday, and I would have to have everything ready for a Monday service. Hesitantly, I made some calls and was able to locate the funeral home I considered best.

My sister arrived later that day. Until then I had felt very alone and frightened. These were uncharted waters for me, and I had precious little guidance through them. I remember feeling hurt and angry that the men in my life had all but abandoned me. Only one of them would even talk with me about what was happening.

My parents came, and we made it through the funeral. God gave me the grace to sing "When Answers Aren't Enough" by Scott Wesley Brown. Becca was buried the next day, one day before my birthday.

What was happening with my life? I had known the Lord for fourteen years, had attended a good church and had been exposed to solid Bible teaching. Why was everything going so wrong for me? Why was my life falling apart?

The timing of the entire series of events had been eerie. Becca's illness had been diagnosed at Thanksgiving in 1987. By March, when her birthday came, her leukemia seemed to be in remission, but by Father's Day we were told that it had returned with a vengeance. I had moved out of the house on my mother's birthday, and now I had no cause to celebrate my own birthday. Every holiday seemed to have tragedy associated with it.

It would get worse. I received a notice in December that Becca's headstone would be installed on Christmas Eve. Someone evidently thought they were doing me a great favor, but the news just tore at my heart. "Merry Christmas, Roger," I thought to myself.

The final blow came when I was notified that a divorce hearing was set for Becca's birthday. I saw no reason to ask that the date be changed, since every other important day in my life had already been trashed. I felt just like Job.

All of this was taking a physical and emotional toll on me. Like most who face the death of a loved one, I had not been eating or sleeping well since Becca's illness had been diagnosed. I wanted to run, in the worst sort of way, but I carried on for the sake of my two remaining children.

Where faith was concerned, I knew only two things at this point. I was certain that God loved me, but I was angry and demanded some answers from Him. I reacted just like Job did. I got "in God's face" and told Him everything I was thinking and feeling. I stopped going to church and listening to any teaching or preaching. I was tired of pat answers, and I wanted to hear directly from God for myself. If my life was falling apart, I wanted to know why.

The day after Becca's funeral, I went back to work. This shocked my co-workers, but I had spent ten months living the tragedy. I explained to them that what I needed at that moment was to do something other than think about Becca and her suffering twenty-four hours a day. Going back to work was the smartest thing I could have done.

Nevertheless, the next five years went by in a blur, and I spent a lot of time alone, trying to find answers to my seemingly elusive questions. Although I did avoid the common pitfall of alcohol or drugs, I made plenty of other mistakes.

The eerie timing of events continued. When exactly two years had passed, I was laid off from the company where I had been working for more than eleven years. Oddly, this provided an unexpected blessing.

Shortly after that, I made the decision to begin donating blood platelets at the hospital where Becca had died. At first it was very difficult to go back there, but I knew I needed to, in order to conquer my fears. Soon the hospital was calling me several times a month. One day the Donor Center coordinator said, "Our little girl needs your platelets." When I asked what she meant by that, she explained that a five-year-old girl had reacted to everyone's platelets but mine, so I had become her only donor.

Through very special circumstances, I was allowed to meet this very lovely young lady and her family. I soon came to realize that God was allowing me to help save a life in return for the one I had lost. Being part of that miracle demonstrated His love for me and renewed my faith in Him.

This did not mean an end of tragedy for me. On my forty-first birthday, my Dad passed away. He had been on kidney dialysis for months and was in a great deal of pain. I knew that I now had two fathers in Heaven, but that didn't make it any easier to lose him.

Things finally began to turn around for me at the end of a ten-year roller-coaster ride that had nearly beaten the life out of me again and again. This all changed, not because life got easier or people stopped hurting me or I had no more battles to face. It changed because I changed. I still recall the moment when God said to me, "Be a victor, not a victim." I came to the realization that I had to throw off the victim mentality I had carried around with me for years. I had to stop living in the past and stop blaming everyone else for my problems.

What changed my life was a profound revelation

from the Word of God that our *response* to life's tragedies determines failure or success. With each hurt,
I had withdrawn more; with each blow, I had fallen
further behind. Now that was all changed.

I owe a lot to a great pastor and great friends. I
thank God that I attend a church where His Word is
preached effectively, where it can penetrate my spirit
and bring hope to my soul. I thank God that godly
men like my pastor and Bob and godly women like
Arlene were concerned enough about me to help me
find my way. I thank God that He was patient with
me throughout my floundering and that He led me
safely to higher ground.

Now I knew that although there would be other
battles along the way, I could overcome and be victorious — no matter what came my way. I wasn't
under the mistaken notion that I could avoid pain
and suffering, but I knew that I could maintain my
faith *through* any pain and suffering that came to me.
I had not concluded that I was suddenly perfect and
would never make another mistake, but I now knew
that when I did I could get up and march onward.
And I had the assurance that failures would now be
fewer and farther between.

My past was so complicated and so painful that I
couldn't bear to think about it, but now I understood
that the past was passed and that it was *today* that I
was responsible for. I couldn't alter the past or guar-

antee the future, but I could live victoriously TO-DAY, and that's the choice I made.

People would still hurt me; I might lose friends, family members, a job or possessions; and I was certainly going to fail. But whatever came, I now refused to be a victim. I would be a victor.

Moses said it best:

> *This day I call heaven and earth as witnesses against you that I have set before you life and death, blessings and curses. Now choose life, so that you and your children may live.*
>   Deuteronomy 30:19 (NIV)

I had chosen life, and the victory that comes with that choice began to manifest itself in my life.

Several months later, God instructed me to write a book about my experience and gave me an outline for it. I had never approached a subject in this way before, but I could sense that this was clearly from Him. Hurting people needed to hear from someone who had been victimized and yet had learned to overcome tragedy.

Over the next eighteen months, as more trials came my way, I put into practice the principles God was showing me in His Word, and they worked. As I applied them and found them to work, I recorded them here. What follows in the next two sections of the book is what God has shown me, what has brought profound change to my life, and what I believe will change anyone daring enough to believe and apply these biblical principles to their lives as well.

Our God is a God of victory, and He has called each of us to live a victorious life, not just when we get to Heaven, but right here and right now.   ✳

Part II

The Victim Mentality

Why is light given to a man whose way is hid, and whom God hath hedged in? For my sighing cometh before I eat, and my roarings are poured out like the waters. For the thing which I greatly feared is come upon me, and that which I was afraid of is come unto me. I was not in safety, neither had I rest, neither was I quiet; yet trouble came.

Job

Chapter 2

Egypt: The Making of a Victim

*And the Egyptians made the children of Israel
to serve with rigor: and they made their lives
bitter with hard bondage, in mortar, and in
brick, and in all manner of service in the field:
all their service, wherein they made them serve,
was with rigor.*   Exodus 1:13-14

Most people would never think of the word *victim*
when they read the account of the children of Israel
in bondage in the land of Egypt. The story of Joseph,
Moses, the children of Israel and their cruel taskmasters is an intriguing one, from start to finish. And
it is surprising, given the circumstances, that little
thought, if any, is given to these people as victims
of the self-centered, power-hungry ruling class, or
even as victims of their own shortsightedness and
lack of trust in God. They were not victims, though

they acted the part perfectly. In the mind of God, they were victors. And we must learn something from them.

Jealousy: The Tempter

The story begins with the young and zealous Joseph. He was sold into slavery, but through a series of miracles he was raised up to take the second highest position in all of Egypt. We marvel sometimes, and rightly so, at the hand of God that elevated Joseph to a place of such honor and favor. His authority was then used to save God's people during a time of great famine. Joseph would later say to his brothers, *"God sent me before you ... ."*

But Goshen was not the God-given birthright of the sons of Jacob; Canaan was. Much of what transpired over the next four hundred years was God bringing them back to the Promised Land.

At our first glance, it appears that Israel was just being taken advantage of in Egypt, an innocent group of bystanders caught in the wrong place at the wrong time. A closer look reveals the steps that led to the victimization of not just one, but millions of God's chosen race of people. When, in reality, God had a great plan for them all.

Again, it all began with Joseph and with his brothers:

> *Come, and let us sell him to the Ishmeelites,*
> *and let not our hand be upon him; for he is our*
> *brother and our flesh. And his brethren were*
> *content. Then there passed by Midianites mer-*
> *chantmen; and they drew and lifted up Joseph*
> *out of the pit, and sold Joseph to the Ishmeelites*
> *for twenty pieces of silver: and they brought*
> *Joseph into Egypt.*   Genesis 37:27-28

Joseph was clearly anointed by God, and his brothers saw him as a threat, so they sought to somehow
eliminate him without getting their own hands dirty
in the process. Unfortunately, it is never possible to
attack God's plans and escape the sight and smell
of the bloody consequence. This is the first step that
places us in a position to be victimized. It may not
be you or I who makes the decision, but somewhere,
somehow, a decision is made that sets the stage for
disaster. Maybe it is our parents or someone else in
a position of trust, a thief who steals from us or even
kills to eat, drink or get high, a driver who fuels his
car with gasoline and his blood with alcohol, a
spouse who runs to the arms of another while ours
lie empty and cold at our sides. The list goes on and
on, but the theme remains the same. Life is not always fair, and it is easy to become a victim — if we
choose to let it happen.

Why even bring these points up, some might wonder, when these things seem so far from our control? The answer is that we set ourselves up to be victimized when we fail to recognize how we are being drawn in by others. This is made clear in the next two verses:

> *And Reuben returned unto the pit; and, behold,*
> *Joseph was not in the pit; and he rent his clothes.*
> *And he returned unto his brethren, and said,*
> *The child is not; and I, whither shall I go?*
> Genesis 37:29-30

Reuben had originally lobbied for *"the pit"* (verse 22), but failed to see the strength of his brothers' convictions or the depth of their jealousy. Time after time, we tell ourselves that we have the answer, that we can change our brothers, that what they're attempting to do will not come to pass. But time and again, we find ourselves devastated when we're betrayed by those we have trusted. We see their dangerous patterns of behavior, but we turn our backs to them, often because they're too painful to face. Our need for love is so strong that we bypass God's plan in exchange for acceptance by others. Sometimes we just think they'll change, or worse yet, that we can change them.

We need to face the truth that many victims are left in the paths of people whose hearts are not turned toward God. Reuben did not confront the evil of his brothers; rather he tried to circumvent its inevitable result. He arrogantly believed that he could safely return Joseph to his father (see verse 22). Instead, Reuben tore his clothing in mourning because his brother was lost.

This cold but simple act of jealousy set the stage for an entire nation to suffer the cruel bondage of Egypt, and it is just that easy for us to fall into victimization today. We're told in scripture that each of us is tempted when we're *"carried away"* by our own lusts (James 1:14). Victims inevitably lie in our wake when we choose to take that which is not ours, as we ourselves become victims when we *possess* that which does not belong to us. These acts place us outside the protective covering of our Father, and like the prodigal son, our fate now rests with the crowd we hang with.

Rebellion: The Crowd-Pleaser

All too often we look for others to blame for the mess we're in. It's as though we secretly know that they will provide just the scapegoat we need to avoid facing our shortcomings. In a way, this is a form of rebellion. Taking a stand against *"every high thing that exalteth itself against the knowledge of God"* is rarely the easy part. We lose our popularity and maybe even the chance to be loved by that one person we feel we so desperately need to fill the void in our lives. When we later sit in the mire of destruction, we point to others as the source of our shame. Instead, we should recognize that their acts of rebellion are just God's proving ground for us.

Paul wrote that *"love NEVER fails"* (1 Corinthians 13:8). I recall the first time I *really* read that! I was convinced that God had made a serious error or that the translator didn't read the scrolls correctly. In my mind, I had pictured the great men and women of faith that I knew or had heard of, and was certain that *faith* was the godly quality that would assure me of success. After all, if most of us were honest, we'd admit that we believe faith is our greatest struggle, and therefore our greatest need (along with patience, of course). But God says *"LOVE never fails."* I realized that His love would always cause and enable me to see others (and myself) the way He does. I would be left with no excuses, just mistakes and character flaws that He died to redeem. If I walk in love, I am guaranteed to be successful in spite of what others may do to me, because I am assured that He will never leave me or forsake me.

It is when I rebel against God's wishes that I become a victim. We'll look more at this in the next chapter, but I'll say this much now. Rebellion places us in a position to be tormented by Satan and by

agwell, preaches a lot about
ch certainly applies here.
th your umbrella when it's
et. It's just that simple.
 in rebellion, and their re-
in and eventually to Egypt,
 Land.
arn that Abraham had once
ypt and back again to what
that I will show thee" (Gen-
 Abraham lied about Sarai
th Lot, and then witnessed
 and Gomorrah. That event
wife.

Egypt, although God used
of His people. The Prom-
ised Land was always in Canaan. That's why it's so
important to see what rebellion does to us. It takes us
from what God says we are and have, to what at best
we settle for or, at worst, leads us into bondage.

Right about now, some of you are thinking that
I'm not being fair to those who have been "innocent" victims of someone else's failure, and many
of you reading this book have been "innocent" victims yourselves. Let me assure you that I care very
much and that I'm not saying that your pain is the
direct result of *your* jealousy or open rebellion. In
Jesus' day, some people made that assumption fre-
quently, and Jesus rebuked them for it.

No, you who have been victimized by someone else do not have a scarlet letter on your chest. What I am saying is that rebellion is one part of a process that produces victims. Sometimes the sin is another's, but the result is the same. And, whoever is to blame, I am convinced that we need to stand against victimization and pray for those who are in its grip. Otherwise, we're headed for Egypt.

Bondage: The Victimizer

Now there arose up a new king over Egypt, which knew not Joseph. And he said unto his people, Behold, the people of the children of Israel are more and mightier than we: come on, let us deal wisely with them; lest they multiply, and it come to pass, that, when there falleth out any war, they join also unto our enemies, and fight against us, and so get them up out of the land. Therefore they did set over them taskmasters to afflict them with their burdens. And they built for Pharaoh treasure cities, Pithom and Raamses. But the more they afflicted them, the more they multiplied and grew. And they were grieved because of the children of Israel. And the Egyptians made the children of Israel to serve with rigor: and they made their lives bitter with hard bondage, in mortar, and in

brick, and in all manner of service in the field:
all their service, wherein they made them serve,
was with rigor.   Exodus 1:8-14

Have you ever met someone in bondage? More importantly, have you ever been in bondage? Are you even now in bondage perhaps? If your answer to any of these is yes, then you understand the above passage of scripture all too well.

I'm convinced beyond any doubt that a Christian in spiritual bondage has been overcome by fear of someone or something weaker than he or she is (in Christ). This is the true harvest of bondage: slavery to that which keeps us from being who God says we are. Rarely is it based on a physical limitation; rather, it is rooted and grounded in a failure mentality. Satan and those he controls know that the only chance they have to defeat us is to deceive us.

This mentality is much more than a "sometimes" thing. It becomes a lifestyle of unforgiveness, a lack of grace and frustrated communication with our God and heavenly Father, a total absence of vision, and broken dreams and submission to sin — all because we're in bondage to a force that was never designed to and is never strong enough to weaken us, much less render us powerless. There seems to be no victory on the horizon because there is no end in sight to our misery and pain.

At this point, men and women become victims of jealousy, rebellion and the inevitable bondage that follows. But it doesn't have to end this way.

Complacency: The Dream Killer

> *Now the Israelites settled in Egypt in the region of Goshen. They acquired property there and were fruitful and increased greatly in number.*   Genesis 47:27 (NIV)

> *... but the Israelites were fruitful and multiplied greatly and became exceedingly numerous, so that the land was filled with them.*
> Exodus 1:7 (NIV)

Look at Israel in this time frame — saved from starvation and basking in Joseph's prosperity. The prophecy to Abraham seems far away. We're not told this, but I believe complacency had set in. It usually does. God saves us from destruction and puts us on solid ground. We haven't possessed our prophetic promise yet, but we're safe for now. So why stir things up? We're in a zone of comfort, and God is providing our needs.

As I am writing this portion of the book, Pastor Bagwell is in the middle of a series of messages entitled "The Seed." What a revelation it's been to see the difference between a hundredfold *blessing* and a hundredfold *person*! Israel certainly fits the description of the former. When God blesses us today, we are responsible to multiply that seed for the need of tomorrow. But they weren't thinking about the covenant God made with Abraham concerning the Promised Land (see Genesis 12). They were sitting in Egypt, prosperous and at ease!

Then Joseph died, and in time, so did the prosperity the children of Israel had known for so long. Now a new king was on the throne, one who didn't know about Joseph. He was jealous and afraid, so he enslaved a people that were *"more and mightier"* than the Egyptians. Though God's people had been shown to be capable of ruling Egypt, they wound up being ruled *by* Egypt.

This was the trap of being too comfortable, and it's no different today. We hesitate, and in some cases refuse, to climb out of the safety net that has broken our fall. After finally recovering from some disaster, we sit by our own personal Brook Cherith (as did the prophet Elijah) expecting to be taken care of supernaturally. But like Elijah, we must eventually move on:

> *And the word of the LORD came unto him, saying, Get thee hence, and turn thee eastward, and hide thyself by the brook Cherith, that is*

*before Jordan. And it shall be, that thou shalt
drink of the brook; and I have commanded the
ravens to feed thee there. So he went and did
according unto the word of the* LORD: *for he
went and dwelt by the brook Cherith, that is
before Jordan. And the ravens brought him
bread and flesh in the morning, and bread and
flesh in the evening; and he drank of the brook.
And it came to pass after a while, that the brook
dried up, because there had been no rain in the
land. And the word of the* LORD *came unto him,
saying, Arise, get thee to Zarephath, which
belongeth to Zidon, and dwell there: behold, I
have commanded a widow woman there to sus-
tain thee.*   1 Kings 17:2-9

Are you staring at a dried-up brook? Has Egypt
grown tiresome? Even a little? If so, you are a prime
candidate for The Deliverer!

Covenant: The Great Deliverer

Years after the Egyptians had forced Israel into
hard labor, the descendants of Jacob cried to God
out of their bondage, and He sent a deliverer to do
what they could have done, had they relied on God's
promise to Abraham:

> *And it came to pass in process of time, that the*
> *king of Egypt died: and the children of Israel*
> *sighed by reason of the bondage, and they cried,*
> *and their cry came up unto God by reason of*
> *the bondage. And God heard their groaning,*
> *and God remembered his covenant with Abra-*
> *ham, with Isaac, and with Jacob. And God*
> *looked upon the children of Israel, and God had*
> *respect unto them.*   Exodus 2:23-25

Always before them was the covenant. God never forgot His word to them, though they had and would many times. But, you see, bondage *always* takes its toll. It begins as a seed planted in our hearts, minds and spirits saying "this is what's right" and "that's the best we can hope for." Israel went away from the land *"flowing with milk and honey"* to a land flowing with seed and money, and when the favor ran out, so did their hope. They had no direction, no vision, and without *"vision, the people [will] perish"* (Proverbs 29:18).

Think about it. Many years would pass before God would send Moses back to deliver the people. In the meantime, day and night the Israelites were made to do hard labor for their taskmasters. Their lives held no joy and no peace, only pain, abuse and the survival of the fittest. Where was God in all this?

Didn't He care anymore? Didn't He see the suffering they were enduring?

Do these questions sound familiar? Bondage is a thief, cruel and cunning. It robs you of your dignity and hope, all the while knowing *exactly* who you are and what your destiny is in the hands of the Almighty God. Instead, you are made to serve the thief, he becomes your master, and when he is finished with you, you are left a defeated foe, caught forever in his grip. All we need to do is look at these children of Israel to understand. Even as they marched out of Egypt with the king's gold in their wagons, they were still ripe for defeat. In Egypt they had developed (and perfected) a victim mentality.

There is hope. Our Father in Heaven is faithful, even when we're not (see 2 Timothy 2:13). He is ready, willing and able to complete the good work He has begun in us (see Philippians 1:6), all because of His covenant with us, a covenant He made and then sealed with the precious blood of His Son Jesus. It is the truth that shall make us free.

It Will Get Worse Before It Gets Better

And Pharaoh commanded the same day the taskmasters of the people, and their officers, saying, Ye shall no more give the people straw to make brick, as heretofore: let them go and gather straw for themselves. And the tale of the bricks, which they did make heretofore, ye shall lay upon them; ye shall not diminish ought thereof: for they be idle; therefore they cry, saying, Let us go and sacrifice to our God. Let there more work be laid upon the men, that they may labor therein; and let them not regard vain words.

And the officers of the children of Israel did see that they were in evil case, after it was said, Ye shall not minish ought from your bricks of your daily task. And they met Moses and Aaron, who stood in the way, as they came forth from Pharaoh: and they said unto them, The LORD *look upon you, and judge; because ye have made our savor to be abhorred in the eyes of Pharaoh, and in the eyes of his servants, to put a sword in their hand to slay us.*

Exodus 5:6-9 and 19-21

One final note before we move on to the next chapter: When God hears our cry for deliverance, be ready for things to get worse before they get better. Satan and our flesh will labor together to sabotage God's plan — not to mention those in authority, our coworkers, and even our friends and brothers.

Joseph's great dream, with which we are all surely familiar, became a nightmare at the hands of his brothers, his captors and his boss's wife. Only after walking through these fires would he reach the pinnacle.

David's was a similar case. He was on the run constantly, with only the distressed, indebted and discontented for company before he would see the throne God had promised him (see 1 Samuel 22:2).

Whether it was Noah or Nehemiah, David or Daniel, Peter, Paul or Mary, time and again God's elect have been subjected to ridicule, pain and countless "setbacks" on their way to victory.

Somehow we have come to believe that only "sinners" face these problems, that Christians somehow will escape every trial and test. Nothing could be further from the truth.

I still remember the day and hour that I made Jesus Lord of my life. Chaplain John Ward was the only clergyman available to meet with me that morning. Man, I needed help!

Our talk only took about ten minutes, but it seemed a lot longer. He would later say that I told him more about "churchianity" in five minutes than he'd ever heard before. When I left his office, though, I knew that God had spoken and that I had found what I'd been searching for for so long. The transformation had begun, but I had a surprise waiting for me when I arrived back at my station.

I was in high spirits, when I was suddenly confronted by my supervisor. It seems that someone had told the senior staff members that another airman and myself had been insubordinate or defiant in some fashion. Still, I couldn't help smiling in the midst of this trial. Jesus was more real to me than the accusations being made against us. Later, my co-worker and I agreed that we had done nothing wrong. I didn't realize it at the time, but this was a preview of things to come. Satan does not like it when we choose to follow Jesus, and He is determined to drag us back any way he can.

From that point, the Holy Spirit helped me to move toward my prophetic destiny. The way was fraught with dangerous pitfalls, as it is for anyone who dares follow the King, but to be hundredfold persons living hundredfold lives, we must be willing to challenge ourselves to pay the price for freedom. We must exchange the shackles of mediocrity and bondage for the banner of our Lord *"and of His Christ."* We must choose victory over the victim mentality. ✳

I had fainted, unless I had believed to see the goodness of the LORD in the land of the living. Wait on the LORD: be of good courage, and he shall strengthen thine heart: wait, I say, on the LORD.

David

Chapter 3

In the Wilderness: The Victim Speaks

Those who know me well will tell you that I'm a bit of a movie buff. Like most people, I watch them for entertainment, but I also find a message in some of them. Such is the case with a movie called *The Fisher King*.

The Fisher King is a tale of two men whose lives become inseparably linked by a common tragedy. The first character is an arrogant radio talk show host named Jack. One night a frequent male caller is convinced by Jack that a woman he met is just not his type. In typical fashion, he interrupts the caller to warn him that such people are a product of "yuppie inbreeding and don't feel love."

"They're evil and must be stopped. It's us or them," Jack says. The caller subsequently enters a bar and opens fire with a shotgun, killing seven innocent people.

Three years later, Jack has become a dysfunctional alcoholic consumed by his part in these tragic events. One scene finds him in the process of attempting suicide, when he is rescued by a street person named Perry. The next day, Jack learns that Perry's wife was one of the victims of that fateful night for which he feels responsible. He works hard to redeem himself in Perry's eyes, but finds he must save him first from the attacks of the "Red Knight," whom only Perry (actually Henry Sagan) can see. The Red Knight is the haunting subject of Perry's nightmare of that bloody night. Both men struggle to find peace in the face of tragedy.

After Jack performs a heroic act for Perry, Perry asks him if it's okay to "miss her now." Through helping Perry and his friends, Jack discovers the meaning of real love and compassion. Although Perry retains his new identity, they are able to move forward with their lives. It's a powerful story.

Unfortunately, the Red Knight of that story is alive and doing well beyond screenplays. The frequency of substance abuse, violence in our homes, and corruption in places of authority are all testimony to pain not yet healed and still very real in the twenty-first century. Men and women everywhere are hiding from each other in fear of repeat violations of the past. Still others chase alcohol, drugs, sex, money, power and fame to rid themselves of the demons of insecurity.

Surely, the children of Israel had not yet escaped the consequences of their own tragic history. Even as they marched out of harm's way, their "corporate" Red Knight was not far behind.

Familiarity: The Enemy Within

And when Pharaoh drew nigh, the children of Israel lifted up their eyes, and, behold, the Egyptians marched after them; and they were sore afraid: and the children of Israel cried out unto the LORD. *And they said unto Moses, Because there were no graves in Egypt, hast thou taken us away to die in the wilderness? wherefore hast thou dealt thus with us, to carry us forth out of Egypt? Is not this the word that we did tell thee in Egypt, saying, Let us alone, that we may serve the Egyptians? For it had been better for us to serve the Egyptians, than that we should die in the wilderness.* Exodus 14:10-12

It's appropriate to cry wolf when you're being attacked, but many people see wolves long after they've been run off. People who have this problem become angry when someone tells them to focus on God's purpose and plan for them instead of on the heartbreak of the past. Their problems seem too big not to be the focus of their every waking moment.

The children of Israel were on their way to the Promised Land when their past came back in the form of Pharaoh's chariots. The "wolf," albeit a defeated one, had returned to threaten their newfound freedom. They couldn't see the danger of that yet, for their hearts and minds had not left Egypt, even if they and their goods had.

In all fairness, the children of Israel had a right to wonder what was going to happen to them next. They would have been well within their spiritual rights to pray for wisdom, even to ask Moses for guidance. But they were still wrapped up in confessing the problem, instead of the solution. Four hundred years of bondage will do that to you.

Amazingly, the children of Israel decided that they would rather live in slavery than die in freedom (though they were not actually going to die). This sounds a lot like the old axiom "Better to reign in Hell than to serve in Heaven." How sad! And how many have repeated Israel's words, perhaps only to themselves (or so they thought).

"I can't do that because …"

"Yes, I know You want me to, but …"

We sit in our comfort zones, safe from the future, and hiding in the past. This causes us to miss God's saving grace and delivering power. He had miraculously brought Israel out of Egypt, with a huge demonstration of power in the process. Joseph had foretold it just before he died. Still, the children of Israel were mired in their circumstances and became angry at the man of God who dared to take Him at His word and be who God said he was, so that God's children might become who He had destined them to be.

How typical of the creation to challenge the Creator and the messenger who points us toward Him. We "bombard Heaven" with complaints of people who have betrayed us and how hard it is to overcome, or maybe we just remind God of real pain, physical limitations and our poor financial status. Our frame of reference becomes and remains that which we are familiar with, that which we know.

We do the same to pastors and counselors, explaining our faith in the light of our fears, when it should be the other way around. Faith in God will always shed the light of truth on our sometimes self-imposed limitations. And His truth shall make us free (see John 8:32), free from our past, our pain and our fascination with the familiar.

These are the true enemies of our destiny, for God is with us and for us. We may or may not be on the verge of defeat, but where God is concerned (and involved), we are also on the threshold of victory.

Last-Minute Rescues: A Difficult (and Sometimes-Defeated) Lifestyle

And Moses said unto the people, Fear ye not, stand still, and see the salvation of the LORD, which he will shew to you to day: for the Egyptians whom ye have seen to day, ye shall see them again no more for ever. The LORD shall fight for you, and ye shall hold your peace.

And the LORD said unto Moses, Wherefore criest thou unto me? speak unto the children of Israel, that they go forward: but lift thou up thy rod, and stretch out thine hand over the sea, and divide it: and the children of Israel shall go on dry ground through the midst of the sea. And I, behold, I will harden the hearts of the Egyptians, and they shall follow them: and I will get me honor upon Pharaoh, and upon all his host, upon his chariots, and upon his horsemen. And the Egyptians shall know that I am the LORD, when I have gotten me honor upon Pharaoh, upon his chariots, and upon his horsemen.

And the angel of God, which went before the camp of Israel, removed and went behind them; and the pillar of the cloud went from before their face, and stood behind them: and it came between the camp of the Egyptians and the camp of Israel; and it was a cloud and darkness to them, but it gave light by night to these: so that the one came not near the other all the night. And Moses stretched out his hand over the sea; and the LORD *caused the sea to go back by a strong east wind all that night, and made the sea dry land, and the waters were divided. And the children of Israel went into the midst of the sea upon the dry ground: and the waters were a wall unto them on their right hand, and on their left. And the Egyptians pursued, and went in after them to the midst of the sea, even all Pharaoh's horses, his chariots, and his horsemen. And it came to pass, that in the morning watch the* LORD *looked unto the host of the Egyptians through the pillar of fire and of the cloud, and troubled the host of the Egyptians, and took off their chariot wheels, that they drove them heavily: so that the Egyptians said, Let us flee from the face of Israel; for the* LORD *fighteth for them against the Egyptians.*

And the LORD *said unto Moses, Stretch out thine hand over the sea, that the waters may come again upon the Egyptians, upon their chariots, and upon their horsemen. And Moses stretched forth his hand over the sea, and the sea returned to his strength when the morning appeared; and the Egyptians fled against it; and the* LORD *overthrew the Egyptians in the midst of the sea. And the waters returned, and covered the chariots, and the horsemen, and all the host of Pharaoh that came into the sea after them; there remained not so much as one of them. But the children of Israel walked upon dry land in the midst of the sea; and the waters were a wall unto them on their right hand, and on their left. Thus the LORD saved Israel that day out of the hand of the Egyptians; and Israel saw the Egyptians dead upon the seashore. And Israel saw that great work which the LORD did upon the Egyptians: and the people feared the LORD, and believed the LORD, and his servant Moses.*   Exodus 14:13-31

In the fifteenth verse, we find a rather strange response from the Lord. *"Wherefore criest thou unto me?"* He asks Moses. This may seem "un-spiritual" to many of you, but it sounds to me like the Lord is using the popular phrase "You talkin' ta me?" God wanted Moses to *"speak unto the children of Israel, that they go forward."* This is the job of the pastor or priest, the prophet of God for your life and mine, although it is an unpopular, if not altogether dismissed, view these days that a man or woman could and should be used of God to order our steps and direct our paths. I believe this happens because, once again, our frame of reference is the familiar.

I grew up in a strong Catholic home, but at the age of seventeen I made the decision to seek God elsewhere. Since that time I have met many sincere, God-loving, God-fearing Catholic men and women for whom I have great respect. One issue, however, that I have always struggled with is the role of the priest. Nevertheless, although I do believe that all Christians are members of a *"royal priesthood"* (1 Peter 2:9), I have come to see that submission to spiritual authority is a vital key to success in my walk with God.

This was not always so. Particularly as a man I had a difficult time in the past submitting to someone I felt I could not trust. This was, of course, a failure mentality based on past relationships. Prior to meeting most men, I would assume they were not trustworthy, meaning they were not worthy of *my* trust. I didn't even have to meet them. I was sure they were going to fail me, so why bother?

My friend Bob and I spent a great deal of time discussing this issue, a tough one, especially for men. It is this concept upon which Promise Keepers is founded, and I believe this is the reason they take so much heat as an organization. Submission to authority is one of the least popular subjects of our day. But I thank God for a pastor who hears from Him concerning our divine purpose as a church and as individual sons and daughters of the King.

It is our hesitancy to submit to spiritual authority that many times sets us up to need a last-minute rescue. When we fail to trust the one God has placed as a covering over our lives, we find ourselves always needing a miracle to bring us to victory. Last-minute rescues should never become a way of life for a serious Christian. While it's true that God's work in us is miraculous, we should not always be in the position of needing Him to rescue us at the last minute if we are walking in His anointing.

Certainly, this was the case at the Red Sea campaign. God said to Moses, "Why are you talking to Me? Speak to the people." When Moses did as God had directed, the way was provided, the people all escaped, and the Egyptians took a permanent bath in the sea. This was a great miracle, but the people were too comfortable with God always rescuing them from their self-created problems at the last minute.

When the morning came and everyone saw what God had done, they *"believed the Lord and his servant Moses."* NOW they believed! Were they not paying attention to the plague of frogs, the plague of lice, and the river that turned to blood? Surely they had heard about Joseph and his rise to second in command over all Egypt. This story would have been taught from generation to generation. God had made a way for His obedient servant to overcome and excel, and this was the God the same children of Israel were serving.

Moses had been told to introduce Him as "I AM." That meant "Whatever you need Me to be, I AM that right now! Whatever I did before, I will do again." It would later be said of Jesus that He is *"the same yesterday and today and forever"* (Hebrews 13:8). He is also *"no respecter of persons"* (Romans 2:11).

The people of Israel apparently had known God only through His miracles. He was not yet an everyday, personal God to them. Otherwise, the past would have had no meaning to them. This would be proven time and again as they journeyed toward the Promised Land, as it is too often in our own daily lives. Is He the God of our destiny (destination) or the one who's always putting us on the spot? As we move from the Egypt of our past toward the Canaan of our future, the way is fraught with challenges brilliantly disguised as disasters. We can either complain about the chariots or wall up the water in Jesus' name!

From the Sea to Sinai: Beyond the Comfort Zone

If there's one thing a victim mentality despises, it's being taken from familiar surroundings to the "next level" through the unfamiliar regions of the "forbidden zone." Most of you know what I mean. Someone or something has kept you from accomplishing God's purpose, so He calls you out of bondage *"into His marvelous light"* (1 Peter 2:9). Of necessity, He begins to speak to you about things that need to be dealt with. I would liken these things to three things the children of Israel encountered on "the-Sea-to-Sinai" leg of their journey home:

> *So Moses brought Israel from the Red Sea, and they went out into the wilderness of Shur; and they went three days in the wilderness, and found no water. And when they came to Marah, they could not drink of the waters of Marah, for they were bitter: therefore the name of it was called Marah. And the people murmured against Moses, saying, What shall we drink?*
>
> Exodus 15:22-24

The first thing that was required of the children of Israel was forgiveness. Like the bitter waters they tasted at Marah, we are brought face-to-face with the bitterness of our souls, made that way through the hardening of our hearts. Jesus dealt with this problem continually:

> *And he entered again into the synagogue; and there was a man there which had a withered*

> *hand. And they watched him, whether he would
> heal him on the sabbath day; that they might
> accuse him. And he saith unto the man which
> had the withered hand, Stand forth. And he
> saith unto them, Is it lawful to do good on the
> sabbath days, or to do evil? to save life, or to
> kill? But they held their peace. And when he
> had looked round about on them with anger,
> being grieved for the hardness of their hearts,
> he saith unto the man, Stretch forth thine hand.
> And he stretched it out: and his hand was re-
> stored whole as the other. And the Pharisees
> went forth, and straightway took counsel with
> the Herodians against him, how they might
> destroy him.* Mark 3:1-6

I once heard Kenneth Copeland say that another
way to translate this word *hardness* is "blindness"
or "insensitivity of heart." These are perfect descrip-
tors of what happens when we allow ourselves to
become bitter. We become blind to our own failures
and God's grace in overlooking them. Insensitive to
the needs of others, we cling to the law and our own
sense of right and wrong (see Proverbs 14:12 and
16:25).

Unforgiveness is a sure sign that you have become
a victim. God dealt with me in the past year about
this very thing. It shocked me when He told me one

day that it was okay with Him if I didn't forgive someone. This was no trivial matter I was discussing with Him. It was an incident that caused me a great deal of pain and embarrassment.

Before you judge that it was God speaking, you need to hear the terms of His agreement with me. I could refuse to forgive this person, He told me, if He could do the same with me.

After crying "foul" and laughing for a minute, I understood the Lord's point with more clarity than at any other time or in any other situation I could recall. My Father overlooks a multitude of sins because of His great love for me (see 1 Peter 4:8). And my elder brother Jesus (*"firstborn among many brethren,"* Romans 8:29) gave His life to redeem me from the bonds of wickedness. It would be a miscarriage of justice for me to enjoy His forgiveness and then deny it to others.

Jesus Himself encountered this terribly ungrateful attitude. The religious leaders of the day seemed to have no revelation of the Word of God, only their own righteousness based on the Law. Most weren't concerned about removing burdens and destroying yokes, and thus they criticized the ministry of Jesus. This is always the fruit of bitterness, and it robs us of the ability to see God moving in, around, and through us.

The next issue God confronted the children of Israel with was a terrible deception:

> *And they took their journey from Elim, and all the congregation of the children of Israel came unto the wilderness of Sin, which is between Elim and Sinai, on the fifteenth day of the second month after their departing out of the land of Egypt. And the whole congregation of the children of Israel murmured against Moses and Aaron in the wilderness: and the children of Israel said unto them, Would to God we had died by the hand of the LORD in the land of Egypt, when we sat by the flesh pots, and when we did eat bread to the full; for ye have brought us forth into this wilderness, to kill this whole assembly with hunger.* Exodus 16:1-3

Victims often believe that the suffering of their past is better than the suffering they will endure to follow Him. Nowhere is the sign of a victim mentality clearer than here.

Israel had been delivered from Pharaoh's clutches, but not from the suffering of their Egyptian bondage. It perplexed me why anyone would prefer slavery over freedom, until I began to see the same pattern in my own life and in the lives of others who had been victimized in some way. Leaving the pain of our past requires us to accept responsibility for our future. There is a void that must now be filled.

That's the frightening part. When our spiritual

wells are emptied of bitterness, wrath and anger (see
Ephesians 4:31), they must be cleansed and refilled.
Paul taught:

> *Christ also loved the church, and gave himself*
> *for it; that he might sanctify and cleanse it with*
> *the washing of water by the word.*
>   Ephesians 5:25-26

When God "flushes" our spirits anew, we will be
called to the place He desires us to be. Oftentimes,
the road to our destination leads through the wilderness, a place of solitude where God can speak to
us and teach us to trust Him again. This is the challenge we face then: to trust God when man has let
us down, to follow Him even though we can't see
where we're headed. And this proves difficult for
many.

To suffer at the hands of another justifies the pain
and anger we feel so intensely. To "suffer" through
God's transforming work does not permit us to escape through the door of sympathy. Were the truth
known, we do not trust Him because we secretly
resent His apparent apathy to our previous (or
present) situation. So, like the children of Israel, we
challenge the visionary (our pastor, counselor or
friend). We demand to know where God is and how
He will provide.

Again, the Apostle Paul wrote:

> *I protest by your rejoicing which I have in Christ Jesus our Lord, I die daily. If after the manner of men I have fought with beasts at Ephesus, what advantageth it me, if the dead rise not? let us eat and drink; for to morrow we die. Be not deceived: evil communications corrupt good manners. Awake to righteousness, and sin not; for some have not the knowledge of God: I speak this to your shame.*
>
> 1 Corinthians 15:31-34

Paul said *"I die daily."* Jesus said that today's troubles are sufficient to be concerned about (see Matthew 6:34). Yet we are so focused on the future and what will happen to us that we fail to see His daily provision. Paul was ashamed of the Corinthian Christians because they knew better concerning the raising of the dead. They had been taught differently. His command to them was "Wake up!"

Israel had been taught God's character by numerous displays of His miraculous power, yet they distrusted Him when they couldn't "see" His provision. The change of residence had not changed their hearts. They were still victims, unwilling to pay the price to obtain their prophetic promise.

The final issue they faced was a product of the stops they had already made along the way:

> *And all the congregation of the children of Is-*
> *rael journeyed from the wilderness of Sin, after*
> *their journeys, according to the commandment*
> *of the LORD, and pitched in Rephidim: and there*
> *was no water for the people to drink. Where-*
> *fore the people did chide with Moses, and said,*
> *Give us water that we may drink. And Moses*
> *said unto them, Why chide ye with me? where-*
> *fore do ye tempt the LORD? And the people*
> *thirsted there for water; and the people mur-*
> *mured against Moses, and said, Wherefore is*
> *this that thou hast brought us up out of Egypt,*
> *to kill us and our children and our cattle with*
> *thirst?*   Exodus 17:1-3

Poisoned by bitterness and frustrated by the process of transformation, we conclude that God is not for us after all. We are grateful that we are no longer victims, but we balk at the effort required to be made free from the spirit of victimization.

"If God cared, He would have ..." We want our Father in Heaven to redeem us in accordance with our wishes, not His. Justice is our reasoning, and a pain-free existence is our agenda. This "manna" might be good for someone else, but me? I'm going back to Egypt!

Stuck at Sinai: The Patience Principle

And when the people saw that Moses delayed to come down out of the mount, the people gathered themselves together unto Aaron, and said unto him, Up, make us gods, which shall go before us; for as for this Moses, the man that brought us up out of the land of Egypt, we wot not what is become of him.

And Aaron said unto them, Break off the golden earrings, which are in the ears of your wives, of your sons, and of your daughters, and bring them unto me. And all the people brake off the golden earrings which were in their ears, and brought them unto Aaron. And he received them at their hand, and fashioned it with a graving tool, after he had made it a molten calf: and they said, These be thy gods, O Israel, which brought thee up out of the land of Egypt.

And when Aaron saw it, he built an altar before it; and Aaron made proclamation, and said, To morrow is a feast to the LORD. *And they rose up early on the morrow, and offered burnt offerings, and brought peace offerings; and the people sat down to eat and to drink, and rose up to play.* Exodus 32:1-6

Israel had now reached the place where God was

going to give them new direction, new revelation for their future. It required waiting on Him for His Word to come forth. Intercession, meditation and celebration would have been appropriate for this time. Instead, the victims' rights advocates talked Aaron into betraying the One who had brought them this far. They needed a new God to depend upon.

When they had satisfied themselves that they had the answer, they began to *"eat, drink and be merry"* (Luke 12:19). Impatience had run its full course. This is perhaps our greatest test this side of Egypt. To witness God at work *"both to will and to do of His good pleasure"* (Philippians 2:13) means that this is a *continuous* process, and we must be patient until God finishes with us.

The Lord showed me this principle so clearly this past year with regard to my children. Like most parents, I see them for what they can be and often measure them against that standard. He reminded me that I am a work in progress and that I should remember this fact when I'm trying to shape my children's character. I began to see what He was driving at. Any attempt at discipline must be done in light of the fact that our children have not yet "arrived" (see Philippians 3:13-14).

Because I was impatient with myself and the work He was doing in me, I transferred that to my children. So it is with most of us. We want to forgive and forget the past and to be whole, but not on God's time schedule, on our own.

We can only forgive if we *"bring into captivity every thought to the obedience of Christ"* (2 Corinthians 10:5). That takes time. For most of us, it will not happen tomorrow or next week. Patience is required.

Whenever something looks the same as it did "in Egypt," only a fresh revelation of God's provision can purge our thoughts. To be *"a vessel for honor"* (2 Timothy 2:21, NKJ), we must remove the failures of the past from our thoughts, words and actions (with the help of the Holy Spirit). These failures are the *"vessels for dishonor"* (verse 20, NKJ).

When was the last time you cleaned house from top to bottom and were able to do it quickly? I've been organizing, cleaning and upgrading my home for several months now, and it still won't be done for a long time. *That takes time.*

The real danger in rejecting the work of the Holy Spirit in this area is that we might replace Him with a false god. We would not be the first nor the last to trade drugs, alcohol, sex, money, power, fame or even revenge for God's best in our lives, but this "golden calf" can never remove our burdens or destroy the yokes that keep us bound. These are poor substitutes that will drive us deeper into the victim mentality. Worse yet, they put us into direct conflict with our God and His commandments.

Only when we yield to His prophetic promise, purpose and plan regarding our service to Him will we be truly fulfilled. David said that the Lord first MAKES me lie down in green pastures, then He leads me beside still waters and restores my soul, and finally He leads me in the paths of righteousness. It's a lot like being in the hospital. We're there to get well, but we don't like it. Bed rest and bedpans! Yuk! None of us enjoys that.

"I can run through a troop and leap over a wall. What am I doing here?" some might say. Yet God does His work in His time. Maybe, just maybe, if we wait upon the Lord, we WILL mount up with wings as eagles, we WILL run and not be weary, we WILL walk and never faint (see Isaiah 40:31).

There is room for Sinai in each of our lives. I've been there before, and perhaps I'll see you there the next trip around the mountain.

The River Jordan: The Past Has Passed

And Moses sent them to spy out the land of Canaan, and said unto them, Get you up this way southward, and go up into the mountain: and see the land, what it is; and the people that dwelleth therein, whether they be strong or weak, few or many; and what the land is that they dwell in, whether it be good or bad; and what cities they be that they dwell in, whether in tents, or in strong holds; and what the land is, whether it be fat or lean, whether there be wood therein, or not. And be ye of good courage, and bring of the fruit of the land. Now the time was the time of the firstripe grapes.

And they came unto the brook of Eshcol, and cut down from thence a branch with one cluster of grapes, and they bare it between two upon a staff; and they brought of the pomegranates, and of the figs. The place was called the brook Eshcol, because of the cluster of grapes which the children of Israel cut down from thence. And they returned from searching of the land after forty days.

And they went and came to Moses, and to Aaron, and to all the congregation of the children of Israel, unto the wilderness of Paran, to Kadesh; and brought back word unto them, and unto all the congregation, and shewed them the fruit of the land. And they told him, and said, We came unto the land whither thou sentest us, and surely it floweth with milk and honey; and this is the fruit of it. Nevertheless the people be strong that dwell in the land, and the cities are walled, and very great: and moreover we saw the children of Anak there. The Amalekites dwell in the land of the south: and

*the Hittites, and the Jebusites, and the
Amorites, dwell in the mountains: and the
Canaanites dwell by the sea, and by the coast
of Jordan.*

*And Caleb stilled the people before Moses, and
said, Let us go up at once, and possess it; for
we are well able to overcome it.*

*But the men that went up with him said, We
be not able to go up against the people; for they
are stronger than we. And they brought up an
evil report of the land which they had searched
unto the children of Israel, saying, The land,
through which we have gone to search it, is a
land that eateth up the inhabitants thereof; and
all the people that we saw in it are men of a
great stature. And there we saw the giants, the
sons of Anak, which come of the giants: and
we were in our own sight as grasshoppers, and
so we were in their sight.*

Numbers 13:17-20 and 23-33

This portion of Israel's history is so familiar. They
are poised to realize their promised heritage, but fail
to do so. After all God has done, their vision is too
small, and their adversary is too great (in their eyes).
On the threshold of a dream, the victim speaks once
again.

I like to envision that day ... two men with a staff

between them loaded with grapes, pomegranates and figs. Although we're not told, I also see them with some of the *"milk and honey"* to take back. What a sight that must have been! How exciting for those who watched as they brought forth the fruit of the Promised Land! After eating manna and drinking water for so long, this must have seemed like a feast. (If you've never had a pomegranate, you're really missing something!) In the words of a former co-worker, "This is huge!"

It sort of reminds me of the bride and groom who eagerly anticipate the coming wedding. This is the moment they've been working toward. Through the highs and lows, breaking up and making up, they've made it to their own Jordan River. The day finally arrives, and they are eager to cross over.

But one of them never makes it to the church. Fear sets in. Too much ... Too soon ... Too hard ... The dream turns to ashes, all because the vision went up in flames. It happens many times, when one of the two has not left the failures of the past behind.

This was the case with Israel that day. They had suffered so much for so long that they were weary of trying. Their past failures had dictated their future course. Only an easy victory would suffice now. As we move from our storied past, we must be willing to pay the price required to possess our

God-given future. We may not like it, but anything less will result in years of wandering.

Some of you have been in the wilderness of pain and doubt for far too long. It's time to face your Jericho and come home.

My parents forbade the use of four-letter words in our home. It would do us all good to remember that *pain, past* and *fear* all are four-letter words. Purge them from your vocabulary!

Caleb (and Joshua) saw the giants in Canaan in light of the promise of God. The others saw the promise in light of the giants, and it kept them wandering for years to come. They even lied about the land itself — *"It is a land that eateth up the inhabitants"* (Numbers 13:32). Some of us will do anything to avoid crossing over to what God says we have, to what He says we are.

It is time for your past to be truly passed.   ✳

If we confess our sins, he is faithful and just to forgive us our sins, AND to cleanse us from all unrighteousness.

John

Chapter 4

Judas: The Ultimate Victim

"It just got too hard."
*"It's supposed to be hard. If it wasn't hard,
everybody would be doing it. The hard's what
makes it great!"*

Geena Davis and Tom Hanks

in *A League of Their Own*

Surely it must have been "hard" for the disciples
to follow Jesus, to "hang with the Man," and it still
is. But with difficult tasks come great rewards. That's
just the way it is. Otherwise, anyone could do it. Joseph served God in the face of betrayal and
disappointment. David kept after God no matter
how many times he failed. Each man of faith received his reward, along with a good dose of
heartache.

I can hear someone asking, "Then, why Judas as

an example of the ultimate victim? Why not Joseph, David or even Jesus Himself?" Certainly Judas Iscariot does seem to be an odd choice, but he has been selected for the contrast we will see later. Make no mistake about it, Judas was victimized in a number of ways. The path he chose is the issue we need to examine for application to our lives and the lives of those we endeavor to help who have fallen prey to "the victim mentality."

Judas as Disciple

Now the names of the twelve apostles are these; The first, Simon, who is called Peter, and Andrew his brother; James the son of Zebedee, and John his brother; Philip, and Bartholomew; Thomas, and Matthew the publican; James the son of Alphaeus, and Lebbaeus, whose surname was Thaddaeus; Simon the Canaanite, and Judas Iscariot, who also betrayed him.

Matthew 10:2-4

We have very little dialog in the Bible about Judas to paint a clear picture of his character. The only additional insight we have occurs within the context of the apostles' involvement in the ministry of Jesus. When we scroll through the testament that contains the life of Jesus of Nazareth, we realize that

Judas must have seen the many signs and wonders the Master performed. As a member of Christ's ministry team, he would have witnessed the healing of the sick, the raising of Lazarus from the dead, and the feeding of the five thousand. He would have been there when the tenth leper who had been cleansed returned to give thanks, when the centurion's servant was healed with just a word from Jesus, and when Peter's nets were overloaded by the miraculous catch of fish.

Judas must have been an unsettled man, a man with not only a hidden agenda, but also a lack of revelation with regard to everything Jesus said and did. Perhaps, in that regard, he is not very different from us.

I wonder what Judas thought when Jesus said *"I have come that they might have life, and that they might have it more abundantly."* Did he really comprehend the depths of that word *abundant*? When Jesus prefaced this statement with the words *"The thief comes only to steal and kill and destroy"* (NIV), did Judas feel much condemnation? He was, after all, stealing from the money bag.

What was Judas thinking when his Boss challenged the Pharisees? Did he know that Jesus was the Son of God, or did he view Him as a demented and self-absorbed man? Was this his conclusion at the Temple when Jesus turned over the tables and drove out the money changers with a whip?

The fig tree, the pool at Bethesda, the woman at the well ... Demons into pigs and water into wine ... Sins forgiven and lives transformed ... In person or not, Judas was exposed to it all. And yet ...

Jesus continually said that He was *"about [His] Father's business,"* but all the while Judas must have been about his own. Perhaps he was lured by the thought of fame and fortune and so went along with Jesus until the going got tough. When his Leader and Mentor talked of His own death, Judas may have decided it was no longer worth it. Or maybe he just got scared.

We're not told exactly what went wrong with Judas, except that Satan entered into his heart, at which point he sought to betray his Master and Friend:

> *While Jesus was in Bethany in the home of a man known as Simon the Leper, a woman came to him with an alabaster jar of very expensive perfume, which she poured on his head as he was reclining at the table.*
>
> *When the disciples saw this, they were indignant. "Why this waste?" they asked. "This perfume could have been sold at a high price and the money given to the poor."*
>
> *Aware of this, Jesus said to them, "Why are you bothering this woman? She has done a beautiful thing to me. The poor you will always have*

*with you, but you will not always have me.
When she poured this perfume on my body, she
did it to prepare me for burial. I tell you the
truth, wherever this gospel is preached throughout the world, what she has done will also be
told, in memory of her."*

*Then one of the Twelve — the one called Judas
Iscariot — went to the chief priests and asked,
"What are you willing to give me if I hand him
over to you?" So they counted out for him thirty
silver coins. From then on Judas watched for
an opportunity to hand him over.*

Matthew 26:6-16 (NIV)

*Six days before the Passover, Jesus arrived at
Bethany, where Lazarus lived, whom Jesus had
raised from the dead. Here a dinner was given
in Jesus' honor. Martha served, while Lazarus
was among those reclining at the table with him.
Then Mary took about a pint of pure nard, an
expensive perfume; she poured it on Jesus' feet
and wiped his feet with her hair. And the house
was filled with the fragrance of the perfume.
But one of his disciples, Judas Iscariot, who was
later to betray him, objected, "Why wasn't this
perfume sold and the money given to the poor?
It was worth a year's wages." He did not say
this because he cared about the poor but because*

> *he was a thief; as keeper of the money bag, he*
> *used to help himself to what was put into it.*
>   John 12:1-6 (NIV)

At this point we get our first insight into Judas' thoughts and motives. He was visibly upset that money was "wasted" on something he viewed to be trivial. Even more so, he likely resented Jesus embarrassing him in front of the others. So Judas set out to hand Jesus over to the Sanhedrin and to collect his wages another way.

This relates back to the first chapter when we talked about jealousy. Whatever it was that Judas really wanted, he came to the conclusion that Jesus was not the answer. This teacher, this prophet, was not what He appeared. The Kingdom He preached was different, so different that Judas was unable to comprehend it. Like us, he needed the Holy Spirit to understand the work of the Father being accomplished through the Son.

So when Judas saw Jesus being ministered to at the expense (literally) of "the ministry," he was livid. Surely the welfare of their team (and his own pockets) was more important than Jesus' feet being anointed with expensive perfume.

This is the danger we all face in serving God, in being His disciples. When He is headed in a direction that we find unpalatable, we balk. We cry foul and refuse to follow, and if our attitude remains unchecked, we abandon our service to Him and sell out to the answer that feels right.

In other words, we become victims of our own self-righteousness and resentment of the price tag attached to God's call. His ways are *"higher than our ways,"* His thoughts *"higher than our thoughts"* (Isaiah 55:9), but the victim mentality never sees it that way. Even before the Spirit of God "gets rolling," victims are filled with doubt and fear, emotions that can and will sabotage the purpose of God. Because people are skeptical of anything that poses a risk to their physical, financial or emotional well-being, they are unable to act upon that which would impact their spiritual well-being. And if a spiritual leader or mentor has let them down, they are even more prone to give up.

Certain that they will fail, they inevitably do.

Judas as Thief

> ... he [Judas] was a thief; as keeper of the money bag, he used to help himself to what was put into it.　　　　John 12:6 (NIV)

Judas robbed God of what was rightfully His. You may debate with me on this point, but a victim always sees his need before the needs of others, and he sees it as more important than the needs of others. This is the person who gets upset when the pastor or Sunday school teacher "ignores" him at church. His pain is so real to him, it *must* be real to others. When Pastor meets with someone else or passes him in the prayer line, the victim spirit takes over. He becomes angry, indignant and impossible to reach.

How sad! How *really* sad! If we could just see the needs of others first (see Philippians 2:3-4), we would catch a vision of God's *"power toward us who believe"* (Ephesians 1:19). I'm not saying that we should deny our circumstances, but that we should see ourselves as victors, not victims, and then move toward that end. Otherwise, we rob our Father of what He would do for, in, and through us.

I dedicate an entire chapter to this later, but I'll share this much now. I was so lacking in this area that it sometimes hurts just to think about it. How selfish I was being, how thoughtless when others needed ministry more than I! The cesspool of doubt, pain and fear was my dwelling place far too often. Fresh springs of living water flow from the mountains above, yet I was too self-focused to scale the cliffs and rid myself of my past beneath the cleansing power of God. Instead of being transformed into a citizen of the Kingdom of light, I sat in darkness, waiting for Him to transform my circumstance.

But I've learned that it doesn't work that way with my Father. His call is always upward and outward, to be and to do more than we have been and done before. That which He gives us is not just for us, but for others to receive through us. In order for that to occur, we cannot afford to "dip into the till." We are to be His "cup," filled to overflowing in order to bless a thirsty and dying world.

This is why victims don't tithe. They refuse to see beyond their own need to the needs of others. Oh, they have plenty of reasons: lack of trust, lack of vision, or plain old lack of resources. But if we are to be His messengers, we must defeat the thief. We must find and follow the path that leads to an abundant life. We must die to self, the self that has become the victim.

Judas as Traitor

While he was still speaking a crowd came up, and the man who was called Judas, one of the Twelve, was leading them. He approached Jesus to kiss him, but Jesus asked him, "Judas, are you betraying the Son of Man with a kiss?"
Luke 22:47-48 (NIV)

If it seems to you that Jesus was the victim in this circumstance, you would be correct in your assumption. Indeed, He was betrayed by a member of His own staff, someone He had taught and trusted. He was totally innocent, yet someone sold Him out to those who hated Him and wanted to put to death the move of God.

But it is equally true that Judas had been made a victim:

> *When Judas, who had betrayed him, saw that Jesus was condemned, he was seized with remorse and returned the thirty silver coins to the chief priests and the elders. "I have sinned," he said, "for I have betrayed innocent blood." "What is that to us?" they replied. "That's your responsibility."*
>
> *So Judas threw the money into the temple and left. Then he went away and hanged himself.*
>
> *The chief priests picked up the coins and said, "It is against the law to put this into the treasury, since it is blood money." So they decided to use the money to buy the potter's field as a burial place for foreigners. That is why it has been called the Field of Blood to this day.*
>
> Matthew 27:3-8 (NIV)

This is why I believe that Judas was the ULTIMATE victim. Once he realized what he had done and the victim mentality had completely infiltrated his innermost being, he committed suicide. Judas had become a traitor, and in his guilt and shame, he ran from God one last time. To him, his failure was bigger than God's mercy.

He forgot that Jesus had taught them to pray *"forgive us our trespasses."* The parables of the good Samaritan and the prodigal son were of no use to him now. He would never hear the words of Paul: *"forgetting [what lies] behind... , I press [forward]"* (Philippians 3:13-14) and *"Christ in [me], the hope of glory"* (Colossians 1:27).

Where was the love of his Teacher and Master? Did Judas stick around to hear Him crush forever the victim mind-set by saying *"Father, forgive them"*? From this passage sequence of scripture, it would appear he did not. Alone and afraid, he took that one final step that all victims share the tendency to pursue and "ended his misery once and for all."

But it didn't have to be that way. Judas could have repented at any moment. A decision on his part was all it would have taken — that and the life-changing power of God. All that's necessary to serve Him is willpower — my will and HIS power.

So I ask you today, what has kept YOU from serving God? Have you failed your heavenly Father? Will you remain a victim, or will you have the courage to reject your past and, like the apostle Paul, *"apprehend that for which [you are] apprehended"* (Philippians 3:12)?

The choice is yours: life or death, defeat or victory, victim or victor! ✳

Part III

Becoming a Victor

*For I know the thoughts that I think toward you, saith the L*ORD*, thoughts of peace, and not of evil, to give you an expected end.*

Our Heavenly Father

Chapter 5

Canaan: The Forging of a Victor

And Moses went up from the plains of Moab unto the mountain of Nebo, to the top of Pisgah, that is over against Jericho. And the Lord shewed him all the land of Gilead, unto Dan, and all Naphtali, and the land of Ephraim, and Manasseh, and all the land of Judah, unto the utmost sea, and the south, and the plain of the valley of Jericho, the city of palm trees, unto Zoar. And the Lord said unto him, This is the land which I sware unto Abraham, unto Isaac, and unto Jacob, saying, I will give it unto thy seed: I have caused thee to see it with thine eyes, but thou shalt not go over thither.

So Moses the servant of the Lord died there in the land of Moab, according to the word of the Lord. And he buried him in a valley in the land of Moab, over against Beth-peor: but no man knoweth of his sepulchre unto this day.

And Moses was an hundred and twenty years
old when he died: his eye was not dim, nor his
natural force abated.
And the children of Israel wept for Moses in
the plains of Moab thirty days: so the days of
weeping and mourning for Moses were ended.
And Joshua the son of Nun was full of the spirit
of wisdom; for Moses had laid his hands upon
him: and the children of Israel hearkened unto
him, and did as the LORD *commanded Moses.*

Deuteronomy 34:1-9

The Death of a Hero

I am impressed here with the splendor of the back-drop against which God sets the stage for victory. Living in the Rocky Mountain area helps a great deal to imagine the scene that day. Moses is perched on top of Mt. Pisgah, a "14'er" (a 14,000-foot peak) near Jericho. He sees across the Jordan River and the Plains of Sharon all the way to the Mediterranean Sea. Beneath him the wind gently sways the palm trees, while the inhabitants below bask in the warmth of the noonday sun. The plains are a per-fect green, made rich by God's own hand. In the background are the fields and vineyards, ripe with the fruit of the land. What a breathtaking sight!

This is the destiny (destination) for which Moses

was called, or, more importantly, called out. He sees it within the grasp of his people, but not his own. He will not be going. Though Moses is in perfect physical condition, he dies, setting the stage for Joshua to take over the leadership position.

Growing up, one of my heroes was the legendary Zorro, so you can imagine my thrill when *The Mask of Zorro* was released. For those of you who haven't seen it, Anthony Hopkins plays the original Zorro, who's quickly caught and imprisoned. Twenty years later, he escapes and trains a new and younger Zorro, played by Antonio Banderas. Though Hopkins exacts his revenge on his captor, Don Raphael Montero, he dies in the process, leaving the future of California in the young Zorro's hands. He tells the young hero that there must always be a Zorro, someone to lead the people and save them from tyranny.

I would maintain to you that there must always be a "Moses," someone to point us toward God and rescue us from the evils of this world. There have been many such men in my own life — Tim Bagwell, Bob Murphy, Johnny Tucker, Gary Copeland and my father — to name a few. Each has sown precious seed into my heart that has been a source of life and health to my soul (see Proverbs 4:22).

Yet it was not always this way. Rebellion and anger marked my past. I've taken more journeys through the wilderness than anyone would care to mention. In order for me to cross over into my divine destiny, new thoughts, words and actions were required. And God has chosen new vessels to lead me through to victory.

This was the challenge faced by the children of Israel as they stood on the banks of the Jordan River. Moses was gone, and Joshua was their new leader. To move forward, they had to let go of the past. After many years spent focusing on the victimization of Egypt, they were poised to possess the Promised Land. Had they latched on to Moses and refused change, the victim mentality would have won out.

It's all too easy to use some man or woman as an excuse to fail, but we must press on in spite of the people who have impacted our lives — whether positively or negatively. If we purpose in our hearts to follow God, then we must abandon our dependency on the actions of human flesh and set our feet on His path. This requires laying aside every weight that so EASILY hinders us. Only then will we find the endurance to run the race He sets before us (see Hebrews 12:1-2).

A Call to Courage

*Be strong and courageous, because you will lead
these people to inherit the land I swore to their*

> *forefathers to give them. Be strong and very*
> *courageous. Be careful to obey all the law my*
> *servant Moses gave you; do not turn from it to*
> *the right or to the left, that you may be suc-*
> *cessful wherever you go. Do not let this Book*
> *of the Law depart from your mouth; meditate*
> *on it day and night, so that you may be careful*
> *to do everything written in it. Then you will be*
> *prosperous and successful. Have I not com-*
> *manded you? Be strong and courageous. Do*
> *not be terrified; do not be discouraged, for the*
> *LORD your God will be with you wherever*
> *you go.* Joshua 1:6-9 (NIV)

It is foolish to think that the purposes of God can be obtained like sweets in a candy store. Yet how often we try to get them that way. We slip in and out of church with no commitment, no pain, no cost, no prayer and no victory! I've never heard of a victory without a battle, but we complain just the same when one (or more) comes our way. I'm an old pro when it comes to this, but I have learned to do things God's way.

When James wrote that we should *"count it all joy"* when we encounter trials, I thought he was "nuts" the first time I read it. However, knowing that God is a lot smarter than I am, I made the mistake of asking Him about it. His answer surprised me. Working

in pictures, He showed me an Olympic athlete pre-
paring for what would be one of many "trial heats."
Having grown up watching the likes of Bruce Jenner,
I quickly understood. These competitors risked "the
agony of defeat" to experience "the thrill of victory."
There is no other way! Try to refuse them entry into
just one of their trials, and see what happens. They
live for it.

This is our call to courage. We must face our trials
as "trails." Just reverse two letters, and you have
the Father's plan for us when the enemy roars long
and loud at our determination to cross over. The
path to victory often leads through the lions' den,
but we are overcomers — not in our strength, but
by His grace and in His name. The sacrifice is well
worth it.

My parents were a constant source of strength in
my life. When I was about ten or eleven, I remember going with Dad regularly to the hardware store
in our small town. He loved fishing and hunting, so
we would quickly find our way to those sections.
One of Dad's favorite items was a circular plastic
container full of lead sinkers. The cost was only
about twenty-five cents.

As he turned the top a few clicks to check out the
different sizes, I saw his eyes light up with the an-
ticipation of owning this simple but great piece of
fishing gear. After a minute or two, Dad would pull

out his coin purse (one of those cookie-shaped plastic ones split down the middle of the top), squeeze it open for just a moment and look inside, and then he would turn and say, "Let's go."

I loved my father intensely, so one time I said to him, "Why don't you buy it? You have enough money." I'd seen everything from pennies to quarters in his coin purse, so much that it was bulging.

But Dad simply replied, "That's okay, son. Let's go." And we left.

This scene would be repeated several times in the course of our lives, and each time Dad left without buying anything.

Years later, I mentioned this incident to Mom, and she told me that Dad had always been concerned that he might need the money to buy bread for us. When I heard that, I cried. This was so typical of the sacrifices my parents made to fulfill their divinely appointed call to raise us. More than just understanding the meaning of love, they lived it. This is courage.

So the question for us is this: What will we do when we've come face-to-face with the enemy? Will we seek God's face and ask for courage in the coming battle, or will we retreat to the safety of what we know. To the victor belong the spoils ... and the trials.

Committed!

> *Then they answered Joshua, "Whatever you*
> *have commanded us we will do, and wherever*
> *you send us we will go. Just as we fully obeyed*
> *Moses, so we will obey you. Only may the* LORD
> *your God be with you as he was with Moses.*
> *Whoever rebels against your word and does not*
> *obey your words, whatever you may command*
> *them, will be put to death. Only be strong and*
> *courageous!"*   Joshua 1:16-18 (NIV)

How sweet those words, *"whatever you have commanded,"* would be to most pastors today. Sadly,
they're missing a great deal of the time. Unless, that
is, we want someone to be committed to US. Then
we shout it from the rooftops!

Yet, commitment is required if we are to escape
the victim mind-set. As an act of our will, we must
press forward in His power and grace toward the
victory that is ours in His plan and in His name.
I've said before that the danger in walking away
from anything is the "hole" it leaves behind. If we
don't fill it with something, Satan will see to it that
the past, the flesh and anything else he can use to
defeat us will creep in.

So, what is commitment, really? I like what Kenneth Copeland says about it. He likens commitment

to flying, because you can't get out in midflight and fix whatever is wrong. You are committed to your course. We need to be and to stay committed to living in victory. Otherwise, we're on a sure course to disaster. This means that when we're tempted to slip into self-pity and do things to satisfy our longing to be loved, we must resist *"in the power of His might"* (Ephesians 6:10) and plow through to the finish line. And when we're afraid to go forward because we've been hurt (HOWEVER intensely or often the pain was inflicted), we must stand fully persuaded that He is *"able to keep that which I've committed to Him"* and so march onward in boldness and confidence toward our divine heritage.

The bottom line is: *"Be strong and of good courage."*

Taking the Land!

The part most of us hate about the victorious work God does in our lives is that we must face battles. Some handle conflict better than others, but for most of us, this is what keeps us from living in victory. If it were easy, we could all do it.

Beyond winning a single battle, we must develop a *lifestyle* of victory. This is what Paul meant when he said that we are *"more than conquerors"* (Romans 8:37). I was asking God about this verse once, and He took me back to my childhood.

I don't like conflict now, but I *hated* it back then. I'd seen black eyes, broken bones and bloodshed, and I avoided fights at all costs. If an official would have been present to time me, I might have set some world record in my haste to avoid bullies. Running suddenly became my specialty, and the distance did not matter.

If you have ever been the victim of a bully, you know that bullies don't just beat you up. They humiliate you. It's part of the show they put on to convince everyone how tough they are.

There is one other trait that bullies have that God used to show me the meaning of the biblical phrase *"more than conquerors."* When a bully has perfected the art of domination through fear, he begins to take whatever he wants just by the mere threat of violence. All he has to do is show up, and people give him a wide berth because they know what will happen if they don't. He doesn't even have to fight!

I had seen and experienced this many times, so I knew what God was driving at. To conquer someone or something through a blood-curdling battle might sell movies, but what God intended for us is to be so strong in the power of *His* might that all we have to do is "show up," and the enemy flees from our presence. Hallelujah! So the task we have set before us is not how to avoid a fight, but how to fight *"a good fight"* (2 Timothy 4:7). The question is not "WHY do we have to take the land?" but "HOW do we take the land?"

God has a plan, and we must find and follow it. The walls of Jericho came down when the trumpets sounded and a victory shout went forth, not when the bulldozers roared!

But victims don't want to hear that. They're too tired and afraid — tired of losing and afraid of the pain that accompanies it. However, like truth, our feelings about it don't change it. We need to wage the battle according to God's articles of war (the Word of God), not the plans our carnal minds conjure up. Otherwise, all we accomplish is leaving a trail of victims behind us. There is no victory for God to savor, only pain and heartache from our vain efforts to salvage our dignity at the expense of the dignity of others.

This does not honor God, who in His Son Jesus endured shame and reproach on our behalf. Lest we forget, it was OUR iniquity that was laid upon Jesus. He was wounded for OUR transgressions, that we might be reconciled to His Father (and now ours, praise God!).

But in our never-ending search for justice, we want others to pay the price for what they've done to us, all the while ignoring the truth that Jesus paid the price for all we've done. Mercy is a wonderful thing, as long as it applies to me. When my Father shows mercy to someone who has victimized *me*, I don't like it at all!

In order for us to dwell in Canaan, our own Promised Land of beauty, richness and victory, we must "take" the land. The evil of hatred, lust and unforgiveness must be driven out. The strongholds of the enemy (Jericho) must be pulled down and burned to the ground. Only then we will experience the *"peace that passes understanding."*

The past of Egypt, Sinai and the wilderness must be remembered for what God did, for His burden-removing, yoke-destroying effect. He delivered the people of Israel, as He has and will deliver us in every battle we face.

If the memories of the past break your heart and "destroy your joy," lay them down, pick up your sword (His Word) and take the land! When Jericho's walls loom large before you, trust your Father to show you how to "bring the house down." Nothing can stop the children of God who dare to look the enemy of their spirits in the eye and declare, "I am a victor, not a victim."

Forging a victor from one who's been victimized is a lot like forging a steel sword. It requires the fire and a design in the mind of the blacksmith. In the transforming process, brought about by the Master tradesman, a new strength and beauty begins to take shape. With each blow of the hammer, the child of

God becomes more like He envisions us to be. The grinding wheel hones and sharpens us for His divine purpose. Before we realize or recognize it, we have become vessels of honor, useful to the Master to proclaim victory and set men free in Jesus' name.

Jesus said, *"I am the door"* and *"I am the way."* Then He gave His life to open the door to Heaven and to pave the way to victory. Because of His work, Paul tells us (in 1 Corinthians 15:55) that death has no sting, no victory, and that victory has been purchased for us over death by and through Christ.

So I ask, are you ready to apprehend what you've been apprehended for? Are you tired of the sustenance of manna that has been keeping you alive while you wander in the wilderness, longing instead for the fruit and meat of the Promised Land? Then you must lay down your life (your way of handling things), take up your cross (your past, pain and rejection), and follow Jesus to Golgotha, the place where iniquity died and eternal life was purchased for all who would come. Only there can we find victory over death, Hell and ourselves, for it was there that history's most famous Victim forgave His tormentors and made all that we have in Him possible.

The old rugged cross is more than "an emblem of suffering and shame" or a symbol of great injustice. It was the place where Jesus laid aside His will and His life in exchange for ours. To victims everywhere,

Calvary is our Jordan River. Crossing over cleanses us from all that has contaminated our souls and sets our feet on the side of victory.

This is so whether you've been God's child for a few days, years or even decades. You CAN trust Him to transform you from victim to victor. How can we neglect so great a salvation?   ✳

Henceforth I call you not servants; for the servant knoweth not what his lord doeth: but I have called you friends; for all things that I have heard of my Father I have made known unto you.

Jesus

Chapter 6

From the Wilderness: The Victor Conquers

This has been my favorite and, to some extent, the easiest chapter of the book to write. I suppose it's because I've had so many thoughts about the life and example of Jesus. It's been my focus these past months as I've dealt with the many things that have tried to cause me to remain a victim.

I have no delusions about how I would've reacted had I been on Earth two thousand years ago. The Roman occupation, along with the religious climate of the day, would most likely have been enough to make me doubt Jesus' sincerity, much less His deity. Let's face it, we have the benefit of hindsight and the help of the Holy Spirit. Without those, we may have wanted Him dead, just as others did.

I have given a lot of thought to the ways in which Jesus handled Himself, especially in circumstances where He encountered a victim or faced the opportunity to react like one. In many ways, that's what this book is dedicated to: exalting the name of Jesus, for He is the one who sets men free — not just the important ones, but any man who comes to Him with the need and desire for liberty.

But liberty is an overused and ill-defined word in the vocabulary of many who claim to be His. I've encountered many who believe that liberty means no restrictions, a theory which is *impossible* to prove by examining the life of Jesus. Above all, He demonstrated the meaning of discipline. When confronted with the opportunity to lash out or reject those who had failed, He always chose the Father's way — which was sometimes harsh, but never cruel or self-serving.

To that end, let's examine Jesus' life and see what we can learn from it.

He Knew How to React to Temptation

Then Jesus was led up by the Spirit into the wilderness to be tempted by the devil. And when He had fasted forty days and forty nights, afterward He was hungry. Now when the tempter came to Him, he said, "If You are the Son of God, command that these stones become bread." But He answered and said, "It is written, 'Man shall not live by bread alone, but by every word that proceeds from the mouth of God.' "

> *Then the devil took Him up into the holy city,*
> *set Him on the pinnacle of the temple, and said*
> *to Him, "If You are the Son of God, throw Your-*
> *self down. For it is written:*
> *'He shall give His angels charge over you,'*
> *and,*
> *'In their hands they shall bear you up, lest you*
> *dash your foot against a stone.' "*
> *Jesus said to him, "It is written again, 'You*
> *shall not tempt the LORD your God.' "*
> *Again, the devil took Him up on an exceedingly*
> *high mountain, and showed Him all the king-*
> *doms of the world and their glory. And he said*
> *to Him, "All these things I will give You if You*
> *will fall down and worship me."*
> *Then Jesus said to him, "Away with you, Sa-*
> *tan! For it is written, 'You shall worship the*
> *LORD your God, and Him only you shall serve.' "*
> *Then the devil left Him, and behold, angels came*
> *and ministered to Him.*
>
> Matthew 4:1-11 (NKJ)

Fresh from the wilderness, Jesus is hit immediately with three temptations: *"the lust of the flesh, the*
lust of the eyes, and the pride of life" (1 John 2:16). This
is a well-known and oft-mentioned passage that contains frequent references to Jesus' use of the Word
of God to fight the enemy. However, what I would

like to focus on are the *reasons* He could overcome with the written Word.

First, Jesus had been with the Father, and He knew who He was.

Second, Jesus knew His Father's will and plan for His life, both generally AND specifically. By that I mean He knew what constituted sin and what His divine purpose was on Earth. This is what made Him a victor instead of a victim.

Too often we struggle in both of these areas, and it leads ultimately to our victimization by Satan and by a world that seeks to better itself by degrading others. If we are to overcome the temptations that come our way, we must be assured of who we are in Christ. This is a subject of great debate in evangelical circles — much to our shame.

We should all know what we have and who we are from our Father's perspective. Religion often teaches us that we are unworthy sinners who must ask for things from a powerful but distant God. This is clearly the victim mentality. How sad, considering that God wants to be so very close to us that there is no doubt in our hearts and minds what His will is for us!

God is, after all, our Father. Didn't Jesus say that if we fathers, being evil, know how to give good things to our children, how much MORE would God give good things to His children (see Matthew 7:11)?

And didn't Jesus also pray that we would be *"one"* with Him and with the Father (John 17:21)? That's powerful — if we believe it.

The trouble is that man attempts to understand these things with his mind instead of accepting it with his spirit — which is where the power resides. I've heard the accusations against those who would dare to believe what God clearly says about His children. "They claim they're God!" "They believe they don't sin!" and a host of other exaggerations passed off as truth. The ones they speak of are, in most cases, simply declaring the truth of what our Father says about us.

To illustrate this, I would ask those who are godly, caring parents to think about their own children for a moment. If I walked up to you and declared that your children were not *really* "Smiths" (or whatever your last name is) and told you they had no right to expect you to do good things for them, that they were just dirty, rotten liars who'd sell their own mother for a cheap suit, and that you don't really love them, that your love is conditional on their "being good," if you're a typical parent, you wouldn't even let me finish this tirade before you stopped me in some way (and rightfully so). They *are* your children — faults and all. You *do* good things for them, in spite of the way they treat you *because* your love is *not* conditional. Your children may not be perfect, you say, but they're not liars, and whatever their weaknesses may be, that's none of my business.

I watched my own mother defend us this way when we were growing up. Once, when I had made a nuisance of myself at Mrs. "G's" house, she came over to give Mom an earful. Mom listened politely for a little while, then she interrupted Mrs. "G" to inform her that I was *her* son, that it was *her* job to discipline me, and that *she* didn't appreciate some-one else correcting me. I was smiling and feeling pretty good about the whole thing ... until Mom closed the door and proceeded to chew me out. Boy, could that Norwegian woman put me in line fast!

Yet, this is the same woman who cried many a tear whenever someone else hurt me. It didn't mat-ter who or why, just that *her* son was suffering. My father was the same way. His hand was strong when we were out of line, but his heart was soft when we were hurting. Anyone who messed with us quickly came to understand that our parents were watch-ing to make sure that no harm came our way. They weren't hateful or violent — just protective.

Most parents I know are the same way. So why should we believe that our heavenly Father is any different, especially when we have His word on it that He is not?

I'm not advocating that we excuse our children's failures, rather, as our Father says, that *"love covers a multitude of sins."* Thank God for that! The blood of Jesus was shed so our failures no longer separate us from Him. In our elder brother Jesus, we have a Savior *and* Protector.

Our Father told Jeremiah that the plans He has for us are *"a future and a [bright] hope"* (Jeremiah 29:11, NKJ). He promised never to leave us or forsake us (see 1 Chronicles 28:20). Romans 8:15 tells us that He is our "Daddy" (*"Abba, Father"* is an expression of close relationship).

God is *our* Father, so why argue about it? We are not sinners. We are *"the righteousness of God in [Christ]"* (2 Corinthians 5:21). Our Father is not blinded to our sins, but He is deaf to the accuser because Jesus was made to be sin to cleanse us from our own.

Jesus was fully persuaded of this and more the day He came out from the wilderness. You could not have convinced Him that His Father had abandoned Him.

There is great power in knowing our heritage in Jesus, our Savior. Paul prayed for the Ephesians this way:

> *Therefore I also, after I heard of your faith in*
> *the Lord Jesus and your love for all the saints,*
> *do not cease to give thanks for you, making*
> *mention of you in my prayers: that the God of*
> *our Lord Jesus Christ, the Father of glory, may*

give to you the spirit of wisdom and revelation
in the knowledge of Him, the eyes of your un-
derstanding being enlightened; that you may
know what is the hope of His calling, what are
the riches of the glory of His inheritance in the
saints, and what is the exceeding greatness of
His power toward us who believe, according to
the working of His mighty power which He
worked in Christ when He raised Him from the
dead and seated Him at His right hand in the
heavenly places, far above all principality and
power and might and dominion, and every
name that is named, not only in this age but
also in that which is to come. And He put all
things under His feet, and gave Him to be head
over all things to the church, which is His body,
the fullness of Him who fills all in all.

Ephesians 1:15-23 (NKJ)

To conquer temptation then, we need a revelation
of God's power *"toward us who believe."* Once convinced or fully persuaded (see 2 Timothy 1:12), we
can attack the enemy of our souls with vigor, knowing that our Father will back us up!

Father,

I pray that all those reading this who are bound
by temptation will lay hold of what and who

they are in You. The victory is theirs through the blood of Jesus.

Amen!

He Knew How to React to Sin

Now early in the morning He came again into the temple, and all the people came to Him; and He sat down and taught them. Then the scribes and Pharisees brought to Him a woman caught in adultery. And when they had set her in the midst, they said to Him, "Teacher, this woman was caught in adultery, in the very act. Now Moses, in the law, commanded us that such should be stoned. But what do You say?" This they said, testing Him, that they might have something of which to accuse Him.

But Jesus stooped down and wrote on the ground with His finger, as though He did not hear. So when they continued asking Him, He raised Himself up and said to them, "He who is without sin among you, let him throw a stone at her first." And again He stooped down and wrote on the ground.

Then those who heard it, being convicted by their conscience, went out one by one, beginning with the oldest even to the last. And Jesus was left alone, and the woman standing in the

*midst. When Jesus had raised Himself up and
saw no one but the woman, He said to her,
"Woman, where are those accusers of yours?
Has no one condemned you?"
She said, "No one, Lord."
And Jesus said to her, "Neither do I condemn
you; go and sin no more. "*

John 8:2-11 (NKJ)

In my opinion, the account we have of the woman
caught in adultery is the most amazing of Jesus' entire ministry. It occurred at the Temple, intentionally
putting Jesus at a distinct disadvantage (or so it
seems). The religious leadership continually sought
not only to challenge Him, but to do it with a crowd
around so as to embarrass and further discredit Him.

This was foolish of them because it always back-
fired on them when they took on the King of kings.
They wanted a death sentence, but unfortunately
(for them), they were talking to Life Himself.

In Luke 4, Jesus' purpose is made clear. He had
come to set the broken, blind, bound, and broken-
hearted free. He would later say that He had come
to give *"life"* and that *"more abundantly"* (John 10:10),
and that included the woman caught violating the
Father's command.

There has been much debate about Jesus' initial
response to this case. Many believe that He wrote

words in the sand. Some assert that He was record-
ing the sins of the accusers. I believe the Word tells
us clearly what He was doing when it says *"as though
He didn't hear."* Jesus was simply ignoring His accusers. Surely, as the Son of God, He knew what
the woman had done already. He had come to Earth
to speak life into all lives.

When Jesus encountered "sinners," His method
and His mission was to set them free. The scribes
and Pharisees wanted only to accuse. This is the victim mentality. Jesus recognized this, and told them
that if they came to judge, then they must be blameless themselves. What a dramatic turn of events! The
Son of God, *the* blameless One, refused to pass judg-
ment; therefore they could not do it either. Instead,
He forgave the woman and told her to *"sin no more."*
Need I emphasize that He is still doing the same
today?

Jesus spoke life to the bound and oppressed and
set the victim free, and although they didn't recognize it, the "religious" crowd could have been freed
as well. More than one victim came to Him that day.
There were many victims present. One of them left
a victor, and the others left angry, confused and
steeped in bondage.

I think my friend Arlene puts it best. She has said
to me many times, "Roger, hurting people hurt others." Sometimes when she said it, I was wallowing

in my own hurt too much to accept her words of wisdom, but she was so right. When our focus is on *OUR* pain, *OUR* rejection and *OUR* loss, we are incapable of forgiveness, and therefore we are bound to do Satan's will.

One of the most profound examples I've heard of this comes from Paul's second letter to Timothy (2 Timothy 2:24-26). Here Paul encourages Timothy to avoid strife, explaining that someone caught in strife has been held captive to do Satan's will. Right now I hear many of you saying "I'm not striving with anyone. I leave people alone." Let's see if that's true.

Close your eyes and take a moment to think of someone who *"has ought against you."* Envision that person standing in front of you right now. If you find yourself becoming angry, hurt and even vengeful, you're still *"in strife."* That person may have been gone from your life for years or even asked for your forgiveness, but still it doesn't matter. You're being towed around by Satan to do what He wants.

You may speak in tongues, heal the sick, raise the dead and be "the man that every woman wants and every man wants to be," but if you don't have love, it's all just a lot of noise in the ears of our Father.

Jesus took authority over the desire to lash out against adultery and responded with the compassion of His Father. Contrary to popular belief, love is not weak. It *NEVER fails*! Forgiveness is powerful. It doesn't just set the offender free, but the offended as well. It is, in fact, too powerful for Satan to overcome.

Father,

Everyone reading this book has struggled at one time or another with forgiveness. Some of them have sadly been the victim of an adulterous loved one. Heal them, my Father, and set them free through the power of forgiveness, which was demonstrated for us at the cross and made available by the resurrection of Christ.

Amen!

He Knew How to React to Injustice

And He entered the synagogue again, and a man was there who had a withered hand. So they watched Him closely, whether He would heal him on the Sabbath, so that they might accuse Him. And He said to the man who had the withered hand, "Step forward."

Then He said to them, "Is it lawful on the Sabbath to do good or to do evil, to save life or to kill?" But they kept silent.

And when He had looked around at them with anger, being grieved by the hardness of their

hearts, He said to the man, "Stretch out your
hand." And he stretched it out, and his hand
was restored as whole as the other. Then the
Pharisees went out and immediately plotted
with the Herodians against Him, how they
might destroy Him.   Mark 3:1-6 (NKJ)

I've been asked many times what causes people
to react the way they do, and my reply is always the
same: they are responding to their *own* sense of justice. In that regard, I'm no different from anyone
else. When we see something happen that violates
our system of values and beliefs, we immediately
label it as wrong. So before you say that YOU would
not have acted like the Pharisees, let's put this scene
in modern context and see if we would be so quick
to side with Jesus.

Imagine a church service ... *your* church service.
Things are going along fine, when Brother Bubba
steps to the microphone to sing. From the start, it is
evident that he is pouring His heart into the song,
but the music and words begin to bother you. It's
country music and you don't like country music, and
the words of the song speak of forgiveness and how
God saved him when he was less than perfect. This
strikes a chord of bitterness in your soul. You remember someone who embarrassed and wronged
you, and you wonder what right he has to sing such

a song, especially considering who he is. Then the words ring out about singing God's praises, and you think, "That's it! I knew He was a radical. We don't need any of that wild stuff in *my* church!"

Just so you know, the song I'm referring to is "Amazing Grace." "I once was lost but now I'm found," and "we've no less days to sing God's praise" are just a few of the words. It is truly amazing all the prejudices we, God's people, still have.

Rap is terrible!
Praise is too radical!
Healing! Well, let me tell just you what I think about all that junk!

The problem is, God has ALWAYS directed us to praise Him, and different people have different ways of obeying that directive.

Paul said that he was *"all things to all men"* that by all means he might win men to Christ. Was he a flake? Certainly not! And Jesus is *"the same yesterday, today, and forever"* (Hebrews 13:8). He never turned anyone away then, nor will He today.

Our view is so limited. Just like the Pharisees that day, we have some carnal expectations (more like demands) about how people should act and think. We're quick to label anyone who behaves differently than we would in a given circumstance, especially in church.

But how did Jesus react to the injustice He encountered in the synagogue? Before Him stood a man in need of physical healing. Jesus wanted to do the work of the Father, but the others saw it only as "work." "Against the Law" is what they were thinking, and He knew it. Jesus was grieved at the hardness of their hearts, as He is today when OUR hearts become insensitive to others.

Jesus responded in two ways: First, He got right to the heart of the matter and challenged them with the question: *"Is it lawful on the Sabbath to do good or to do evil, to save life or to kill?"* And they didn't have an answer. Folks like that never do when confronted with absolute truth.

Then Jesus was moved with compassion to meet the man's need and fulfill the Father's purpose — in spite of what the Pharisees thought and what they were going to do to Him. After all, this wasn't the first or the last time the Pharisees challenged Him. They weren't concerned about the needs of the people, only the empire they were building for themselves. To them, Jesus represented the destruction of all they had done and everything they believed in. We call that politics, prejudice or just plain "unfair," and often we're right.

When people act like this, someone is always victimized in the process. That is why we must do what Jesus did when confronted by injustice caused by others or by the system. To react with demands for justice is to ask our Father to treat us likewise. Do not the Scriptures teach us that we will be measured by our own yardsticks? I'm not suggesting that we ignore injustice, but rather that we fight it with the *"weapons of our warfare,"* which *"are not carnal."*

So how does a victor react to injustice? A victim reacts in the flesh, complete with a demand that the problem be "fixed" and that "an eye for an eye" be rendered. As victors, we look to God to meet our needs and to provide mercy for the one who has wronged us. We are told to pray for those who *"persecute"* us, and to *"love"* our enemies (Matthew 5:44). I see it this way: We must pray for God's best for them. This means that He will be living in and through them, changing their character, and teaching them to be like Him.

Jesus told a parable about a man who hired workers at different times of the day, but paid them all the same at the end of that day. That certainly seems like an injustice to me, yet it is God's prerogative to determine how others will be dealt with. That's none of our business, and I'm glad of that.

We must give up our cry for justice, lest *we* ourselves receive the justice we deserve. We must also be ready to meet the needs of those who are victims of injustice. Jesus could have become angry and stormed out without restoring the man's hand, but

He saw the need as more important than the earthly consequence (His death at Calvary). Perhaps this is what He meant when He said *"deny yourself, take up your cross, and follow Me."*

Father,

Teach us what it means to serve You, to lay aside our "rights" for Your "righteousness," to love as You loved, to pray as Jesus prayed. Jesus, You once prayed, "Father forgive them." The forgiveness You gave us, we must give others. Break our prejudices and transform us into Your image. We ask for Your best, Your very best for those who have heaped their injustice on us and others. For we know and trust that only then will their failure cease. And thank You, Father, for being patient with us when we abuse the rights and dignity of others. Have mercy upon us all.

Amen!

He Knew How to React to Persecution

Then some Pharisees and teachers of the law came to Jesus from Jerusalem and asked, "Why do your disciples break the tradition of the elders? They don't wash their hands before they eat!"

Jesus replied, "And why do you break the command of God for the sake of your tradition? For God said, 'Honor your father and mother' and 'Anyone who curses his father or mother must be put to death.' But you say that if a man says to his father or mother, 'Whatever help you might otherwise have received from me is a gift devoted to God,' he is not to 'honor his father' with it. Thus you nullify the word of God for the sake of your tradition. You hypocrites! Isaiah was right when he prophesied about you:

" 'These people honor me with their lips,
but their hearts are far from me.
They worship me in vain;
their teachings are but rules taught by men.' "

Jesus called the crowd to him and said, "Listen and understand. What goes into a man's mouth does not make him 'unclean,' but what comes out of his mouth, that is what makes him 'unclean.' "   Matthew 15:1-11 (NIV)

"Tradition, tradition!" I can still hear the words echoing around the room at the dinner theater where I had made reservations to see *Fiddler on the Roof.* This humorous play is set against a backdrop of a group of Jews living in Russia in the early 1900s. Sitol has three lovely daughters who proceed to fall in love, breaking the time-honored tradition of "matchmaking." In the end, one of the girls marries a "Gentile," breaking her father's heart and causing a rift to develop between them.

It's sad to see the traditions of men separate people, but, as corny as it may sound, it is traditional for tradition to do just that. Even when godly principles are at stake, men find ways to mess things up and build walls. Our many denominations and the fighting among them are classic evidence of just that.

The Pharisees wanted their traditions adhered to "religiously." Their customs, developed over many years, had turned into a ritual and eventually a rite. Funny how that happens! We begin with good intentions, but somewhere along the way we turn a good thing, with meaning for us personally, into universal law.

There's a very popular saying right now in Christian circles. It asks the question "What would Jesus do?" Often you see this question expressed as "W.W.J.D.?" I've seen it on bumper stickers, lapel pins and wristbands, to name just a few places. Let's use that question to examine the events of Matthew 15.

If Jesus had reacted the way most of us do, He would have accomplished nothing more than to insult the Pharisees and justify the disciples' actions as being insignificant. That's what victims do. But Jesus was always a victor, so He responded with

power and authority. Instead of saying that their tradition was not in the Scriptures, Jesus asked the
Pharisees why they were violating the Scriptures
with their traditions. At first, this may seem to some
like a play on words, but the two are quite different.

The first is a defense of the flesh. It says, "Show
me where the Scriptures teach that?" This reaction
is intended solely to get our accusers off our backs.
Victims do this quite often. We just want people to
stop beating us up, so our only focus is to get rid of
the bully. But our Father has promised us the victory *"by the blood of the Lamb and the word of [our]
testimony."* We, in turn, must always follow His
Word.

Jesus did more than just chew the Pharisees out.
He pointed out the error of their tradition in a way
they would not be able to forget. Remember, He said
that He had come to seek and to save that which
was lost. That meant tearing down everything that
kept them (and us) from victory in His name.

A victor is not afraid to confront things contrary
to God's plan and purpose for our lives. Unlike most,
however, a true victor does not "dice and slice"
people to make them feel worthless. We are commanded to *"speak the truth in love."* This is a powerful
command, one that we dare not ignore.

"But Jesus seemed so unloving," some might say.

Sometimes we need to turn off our religious thinking in order to hear the heart of our Father. Jesus'
love for the people who were being oppressed by
the Pharisees' rules took precedence over the tem-
porary wounds His words would inflict upon
their egos.

This is the secret to speaking in love. We must love
His Word, His will and His plan for others before
we can offer rebuke for ungodly behavior. Otherwise, the victim speaks, justice is demanded, and
heads are chopped off. Then blood is on our hands
and we are subsequently rejected at the altar when
we pray.

We must allow God's love to be *"shed abroad in
our hearts"* (Romans 5:5) so that we can speak truth
without inflicting what could be permanent dam-
age on another life. Like many, I learned this lesson
the hard way. The church I attended at the time held
a youth retreat in the Colorado mountains every
year in the spring. That year, one particular young
man was being very rebellious, and I took it upon
myself to straighten him out. In the process, I used
the Word of God like a sword against his behavior,
and I thought this was appropriate.

In the middle of that retreat, God explained to me
that the *"sword of truth"* in Ephesians 6 was intended
to be used against Satan, not against my brother or
sister. He then gently pointed out that the truth is to

be used like a surgeon's scalpel to carefully and precisely heal the broken heart without causing unnecessary harm. This was shown to me in Proverbs 4:22 (NKJ), where He says that His words are *"life to those who find them, and health [medicine] to all their flesh."*

Before the retreat ended, I apologized to that young man and vowed to my Father that I would never again dispense truth in that fashion. In my zeal for the Lord, I had stepped out of love, and it was an offense to Him.

Like Jesus, we must counter persecution with the truth of God's Word, spoken with love for God and for those to whom we are speaking.

Father,

Teach us how to love, to love You so much that we love all Your creation enough to speak Your truth, as a surgeon skillfully works to heal a sick body. Holy Spirit, take over our mouths that we might glorify our Father with what we speak. And Holy Father, teach us truth, not tradition. Deliver us from evil.

Amen!

He Knew How to React to Death

On Herod's birthday the daughter of Herodias danced for them and pleased Herod so much

*that he promised with an oath to give her what-
ever she asked. Prompted by her mother, she
said, "Give me here on a platter the head of John
the Baptist." The king was distressed, but because of his oaths and his dinner guests, he
ordered that her request be granted and had
John beheaded in the prison. His head was
brought in on a platter and given to the girl,
who carried it to her mother. John's disciples
came and took his body and buried it. Then they
went and told Jesus.*

*When Jesus heard what had happened, he with-
drew by boat privately to a solitary place.*

Matthew 14:6-13 (NIV)

It would be natural here to talk about Lazarus or
even Jesus Himself being raised from the dead, but
most of us don't have the benefit of that viewpoint.
We have witnessed the deaths of those we loved,
and those deaths were sometimes horrible. Experience seems to tell us that the miracle we hope for
does not always come.

At first glance, Jesus' response to the death of John,
His cousin, fellow minister and friend, doesn't appear all that significant or unusual. Maybe He feared
for His life. Perhaps He just wanted to be alone to
sort out His thoughts. Certainly these actions would
be considered normal, even expected.

But Jesus' motive was far different. Once again, He showed us how to be victorious in the midst of pain, sorrow and death. In similar circumstances, most of us would be filled with rage and demanding justice (meaning revenge). Others might have run in fear of what would happen to those who knew John (as we see Peter doing later). But Jesus did none of these things. He didn't plot revenge against Herod, although He could've used His divine power to strike him dead on the spot. Jesus didn't even confront Herod — either publicly or privately, as many of us would have.

No, Jesus did something so remarkable that it still astonishes me to this day. As we read further into the fourteenth chapter, we discover the road Jesus followed to victory over Herod and Satan:

> *Hearing of this, the crowds followed him on foot from the towns. When Jesus landed and saw a large crowd, he had compassion on them and healed their sick.*
>
> *As evening approached, the disciples came to him and said, "This is a remote place, and it's already getting late. Send the crowds away, so they can go to the villages and buy themselves some food."*
>
> *Jesus replied, "They do not need to go away. You give them something to eat."*

*"We have here only five loaves of bread and two
fish," they answered.*

*"Bring them here to me," he said. And he di-
rected the people to sit down on the grass.
Taking the five loaves and the two fish and look-
ing up to heaven, he gave thanks and broke the
loaves. Then he gave them to the disciples, and
the disciples gave them to the people. They all
ate and were satisfied, and the disciples picked
up twelve basketfuls of broken pieces that were
left over. The number of those who ate was about
five thousand men, besides women and children.
Immediately Jesus made the disciples get into
the boat and go on ahead of him to the other
side, while he dismissed the crowd. After he had
dismissed them, he went up on a mountainside
by himself to pray.*

Matthew 14:14-23 (NIV)

Jesus' response to the death of John the Baptist
was to speak "life" into those who came to Him in
need. They weren't asked to come back later or told
that the Master needed rest (as the disciples had
done previously when children approached Him
after a long day). And Jesus didn't just heal their
sick, He made sure they were fed. He completely
conquered evil with good, as Paul would later in-
struct us to do:

> *Do not take revenge, my friends, but leave room*
> *for God's wrath, for it is written: "It is mine to*
> *avenge; I will repay," says the Lord. On the*
> *contrary:*
> *"If your enemy is hungry, feed him;*
> *if he is thirsty, give him something to drink.*
> *In doing this, you will heap burning coals*
> *on his head."*
> *Do not be overcome by evil, but overcome evil*
> *with good.*   Romans 12:19-21 (NIV)

This is the way a victor thinks. Find and follow
God's plan, which always leads to life. Jesus said *"I
am the way, the truth, and the life."* Instead of just tell-
ing someone to get a life, He WAS life. Jesus gave of
Himself always, even in the face of the brutal mur-
der of someone He was very close to.

Matthew goes on to say that Jesus came to them
in the boat while it was being driven violently by
the wind. Immediately the wind died down, and
they crossed over to the other side. Jesus didn't retreat; He advanced to victory by doing the will of
the Father.

"Brother, are you saying that it's wrong to grieve
or to spend time alone to get ourselves together after someone dies?" No, I'm not. I know from painful
personal experience that human flesh requires time
to heal. What I am saying, however, is that it *is*
wrong to remain in grief too long.

The way to conquer the pain of death, Jesus' way, is by giving life to those around us. We have the precious Spirit of God residing in us. He stands ready, willing and able to lead us to victory — if we will only trust Him. Through His grace, we can do things we never dreamed were possible. We can see "life" the way He intended — not just because we are breathing, walking and talking, but because we have God's best.

Unless Jesus returns to get us, all of us will die someday. What we do in the "in-between time" brings life to us and to those around us. Life does not end with physical death. It ends with spiritual death! To be separated from the One who formed us, preserved us, loved us and then died for us would be the real tragedy.

Our Father tells us that the death of one of His saints is *"precious"* to Him (Psalm 116:15). He rejoices at their homecoming. That's tough, I know. As the popular saying is, "Been there! Done that!" God wants us to have an abundant life — a life of victory. This is what we have in Jesus, the One who gave life to others when He had just witnessed death. Through Him, we can do the same!

Father,

Reveal Your abundant life to us that we might offer it to others. We repent of our selfishness in serving You. Sometimes we have our own agendas, including our demand for justice when a wrong is done. We forget the way that Jesus dealt with our sin at the cross. Forgive us, teach us, and transform us into the image of Your Son. Only then will we reach the world for Your Kingdom's sake.

Amen!

He Knew How to React to Betrayal

This was now the third time Jesus appeared to his disciples after he was raised from the dead. When they had finished eating, Jesus said to Simon Peter, "Simon son of John, do you truly love me more than these?" "Yes, Lord," he said, "you know that I love you."

Jesus said, "Feed my lambs."

Again Jesus said, "Simon son of John, do you truly love me?"

He answered, "Yes, Lord, you know that I love you."

Jesus said, "Take care of my sheep."

The third time he said to him, "Simon son of John, do you love me?"

Peter was hurt because Jesus asked him the third time, "Do you love me?" He said, "Lord, you

know all things; you know that I love you."
Jesus said, "Feed my sheep."

John 21:14-17 (NIV)

Being betrayed is probably the hardest of all things for us to overcome. Unlike some other ways in which we are hurt, this one comes from someone we counted on for loyalty and support. Most times the betrayal is calculated and premeditated. Sometimes it comes in the wake of difficult circumstances. No matter, the result is the same ... and it *is* personal.

Peter was, to some, merely a victim of circumstance. He was afraid that what men had done to his Teacher and Friend would happen to him as well. No one relished the thought of arrest and trial, least of all the way the Romans did it. Crucifixion was always a most gruesome option.

But this is not the picture we have of Peter earlier:

> *Then Simon Peter, who had a sword, drew it and struck the high priest's servant, cutting off his right ear. (The servant's name was Malchus.) Jesus commanded Peter, "Put your sword away! Shall I not drink the cup the Father has given me?" Then the detachment of soldiers with its commander and the Jewish officials arrested Jesus.*   John 18:10-12 (NIV)

Where was the staunch defender of Jesus now? Perhaps he was confused by the events that had just transpired. Jesus had certainly acted strangely in refusing Peter's help earlier. Then there was the matter of Jesus' prophecies of His own death. Peter had a lot on his mind and, as usual, was not handling things well at all. The net result was that Peter betrayed Jesus by saying he didn't even know Him. How dreadful!

I don't recall anyone ever doing that to me. Most of the time when people betray us, it's what they say not what they don't that does us harm. But a lie is a lie, and Jesus knew what had happened even though He was under lock and key in the courtyard of the High Priest.

Days later, risen from the dead, Jesus had an opportunity to confront one of His two betrayers. He asked Peter three times (one for each time His disciple had denied knowing Him) if he loved Him. Peter replied that he did, whereupon Jesus commanded him, *"Feed My sheep."*

There is perhaps no greater evidence of forgiveness in all the Scriptures, but there is much more than forgiveness here. There is also restoration of relationship based on trust. This is reconciliation. Too often we lump these two together, when in fact they are separate issues. A lack of understanding of this fact can lead to a repeat of the events that victimized our lives.

Jesus KNEW He could trust Peter with the Gospel because He knew Peter's heart. The Holy Spirit was also about to come upon His disciples — an event that would transform them forever. Peter was truly repentant for what he had done, and this is what enabled him to become trustworthy (worthy of trust) again.

We *must* forgive those who have betrayed us if we are to follow Jesus' example and experience His blessing and peace. This will set us free and put us on the road to victory. Perhaps they *"know not what they do,"* and perhaps they do. It doesn't matter. We are forgiven in Christ, and having *"freely received,"* we must *"freely give."* However, we are not required to restore fellowship (reconcile) with the persons who have offended us unless true repentance is shown. To place people in a position of trust in our lives when they have yet to repent of their sin and change their behavior is foolish and will only lead to further harm. We can pray God's best for them without inviting them over for dinner!

Jesus could have done what most of us would have — reject and punish the one who had betrayed His trust. But He didn't, and as a result the Gentiles, of whom we are a part, were brought the good news of His life, death and resurrection. Imagine what it would be like for us had only the Jews received that word!

Father,

When someone has betrayed us and broken our hearts, remind us that You look beyond our own faults to see our need. Make us like Jesus, who rose to victory over death, Hell, the grave ... and betrayal.

Amen!

He Knew How to React to Trouble

When Jesus saw the crowd around him, he gave orders to cross to the other side of the lake. Then he got into the boat and his disciples followed him. Without warning, a furious storm came up on the lake, so that the waves swept over the boat. But Jesus was sleeping. The disciples went and woke him, saying, "Lord, save us! We're going to drown!"

He replied, "You of little faith, why are you so afraid?" Then he got up and rebuked the winds and the waves, and it was completely calm.

The men were amazed and asked, "What kind of man is this? Even the winds and the waves obey him!"

Matthew 8:18 and 23-27 (NIV)

Each of the past two summers I've gone white-water rafting and loved every minute of it. Here in

Colorado, the most popular place to do this is the Arkansas River, where you can raft all the way from Buena Vista to the Royal Gorge. The water is highest in June, when the mountain snow is still melting.

The first year, I was nervous because I had heard it was a dangerous sport, especially if a person becomes careless. I quickly saw why when we arrived at "The Suckhole." Unlike "The Widow Maker" and other choice rapids we had traversed, this was a monster. The drop was at least twelve feet into a hole in the river created by water flowing over and around several large rocks. We all swallowed hard as we watched raft after raft dump their human contents into the raging waters trying to cross "The Suckhole."

When our turn came, we launched our six rafts and headed off to see if our fate would be the same. Thanks to a wonderful guide who urged us to keep paddling so that the raft could not get stuck in the dreaded hole, we made it through without losing a single rafter. I was so excited that I wanted to do it all over again.

Earlier this month, I had a chance to see the ocean again, this time at San Francisco. It's was an awesome sight. Although an ocean is quite different from a raging river, the power of the waves is still very evident. So I can imagine a little of what it was like that day so long ago on the Sea of Galilee as the storm rose and sent large, powerful waves crashing against the ship. It would be normal and even expected to fear death at that juncture. Like *Titanic* on the big screen, it is a very scary experience.

And what was Jesus doing while "all hell" was breaking loose? He was sleeping, taking a well-deserved rest after a typical day in the life of the Son of God. Many of the men with Him were fishermen, however, and they were accustomed to storms and had seen firsthand what one could do to even the best of ships. They were, therefore, probably a little miffed when they found Jesus sleeping so soundly. I think I might have been too.

Jesus' response to them when they woke Him up gives us insight into several things, including the attitude behind their request. He asked them why they were afraid, accusing them of being men *"of small faith."* My response probably would have been, "Excuse me, what did You say? We're going down here, and it's my fault? I don't think so. Besides, I've done all I know how, and we're still taking on water." Jesus' words certainly seemed harsh, considering the fact that the disciples seemed ready to drown. After all, it had been *His* idea to go by boat.

Did you ever think thoughts like this about your boss? How about God? You probably have, especially when it came to something He told you to do and you didn't see how you could possibly do it.

Once again, let's put this situation into its context.
Jesus had been about His Father's business, teaching and healing all who came to Him, including His
disciples. He had just finished healing Peter's
mother-in-law, casting out demons, and healing *"all
who were ill."* Then He had told them to go to the
other side. In other words, they had ample evidence
that everything Jesus said was being directed by
God, and that He had the power needed to back it
up. The problem was, they were still spectators, not
participants.

Jesus wanted them to act on what they had seen
and heard. What stopped them from speaking to the
wind and waves themselves? Fear and the victim
mentality, which always rears its ugly head in time
of trouble.

We need to think as Jesus thought, to see what
Jesus saw, and to do what Jesus did. Think victory,
not defeat. See the finish line, not the obstacle course.
Speak to the things that stand in your way, bringing peace and calm to your circumstances.

Paul prayed this way:

> *Therefore I also, after I heard of your faith in
> the Lord Jesus and your love for all the saints,
> do not cease to give thanks for you, making
> mention of you in my prayers: that the God of
> our Lord Jesus Christ, the Father of glory, may*

> *give to you the spirit of wisdom and revelation*
> *in the knowledge of Him, the eyes of your un-*
> *derstanding being enlightened; that you may*
> *know what is the hope of His calling, what are*
> *the riches of the glory of His inheritance in the*
> *saints, and what is the exceeding greatness of*
> *His power toward us who believe, according to*
> *the working of His mighty power which He*
> *worked in Christ when He raised Him from the*
> *dead and seated Him at His right hand in the*
> *heavenly places, far above all principality and*
> *power and might and dominion, and every*
> *name that is named, not only in this age but*
> *also in that which is to come.*
>
> Ephesians 1:15-20 (NKJ)

It's the phrase *"the exceeding greatness of His power toward us who believe"* that applies here. Strong's Concordance says it this way: "miraculous *power* (far beyond 'great') that has come to us who believe." Wow! That means we have everything we need to face trouble and defeat it.

But victims don't want to do that. They would rather exhaust their own resources and then complain to God when trouble's still camping in their living room and devouring their goods. That is giving up on God and giving in to Satan!

How long will we stand with sword in hand (see

Ephesians 6) and let our enemy defeat us? It's our choice. God is at work in us, *"both to will and to do for his good pleasure"* (Philippians 2:13, NKJ). Victors please him; victims do not.

The writer of Hebrews declared:

> *Therefore we also, since we are surrounded by so great a cloud of witnesses, let us lay aside every weight, and the sin which so easily ensnares us, and let us run with endurance the race that is set before us, looking unto Jesus, the author and finisher of our faith, who for the joy that was set before Him endured the cross, despising the shame, and has sat down at the right hand of the throne of God. For consider Him who endured such hostility from sinners against Himself, lest you become weary and discouraged in your souls.*
>
> *You have not yet resisted to bloodshed, striving against sin.*   Hebrews 12:1-4 (NKJ)

Father,

We are called Christians. Help us live up to all it means to be "followers of Christ." As He conquered, so let us conquer. As He spoke, so let us speak. As He lived, so let us live.

Amen!

✳

Brethren, I do not count myself to have apprehended; but one thing I do, forgetting those things which are behind and reaching forward to those things which are ahead, I press toward the goal for the prize of the upward call of God in Christ Jesus.

Paul, NKJ

Chapter 7

Peter: The Ultimate Victor

In the warrior's code there's no surrender
When his body says "stop," his spirit cries
"Never!"
Deep in our soul a quiet ember knows it's you
against you.
It's the paradox that drives us on.
It's a matter of wills.
In the heat of attack, it's the passion that kills.
The victory is yours alone.

From the song "The Burning Heart,"

from the movie *Rocky IV*

The words of this song still ring in my ears from having watched the saga of Rocky Balboa, a champion who never gave up. Although the character is fictitious, the story is a fascinating tale of courage and love. Each movie in the series has been an inspiration, especially during the times I wanted to give up in the midst of my own struggles.

Notice the phrase, "When his body says 'stop,' his spirit cries 'Never!' " This is the mark of a true champion. Edwin Louis Cole says that a winner isn't someone who never fails, but rather, someone who never quits. This is what I want us to see about Peter. We're all quick to point out his flaws, because that's what we see the most. But Peter became a victor, not because he stopped making mistakes, but because he said "Never!" when his circumstances cried out "stop." He was flawed, but not forgotten, failing, but not a failure. If we can learn from him, we, too, can become victorious.

I've often thought I'm a lot like Peter. At times, I have been impatient and foolish. Conflict is far from my specialty. I'd rather run than fight. But there is hope for me, as there was for Peter ... and for you.

Peter as Traitor

Then after about an hour had passed, another confidently affirmed, saying, "Surely this fellow also was with Him, for he is a Galilean."
But Peter said, "Man, I do not know what you are saying!" Immediately, while he was still speaking, the rooster crowed. And the Lord turned and looked at Peter. And Peter remem-

bered the word of the Lord, how He had said to him, "Before the rooster crows, you will deny Me three times." So Peter went out and wept bitterly. Luke 22:59-62 (NKJ)

In the chapter on Judas, I stated that he was chosen as the ultimate victim to show a contrast, one that we see in the life of Peter. Both betrayed Jesus, but with vastly different results.

The Scriptures speak of *"godly sorrow that produces repentance"* (2 Corinthians 7:10, NKJ). This is what Peter felt. Otherwise, he would not have stuck around. Judas, recognizing that he had betrayed innocent blood, committed suicide. Peter did not.

It takes courage to try again after heartache and failure. Peter was a victim of his own shortsightedness and fleshly reactions. How familiar that sounds! So often in our zeal for the Lord we "shoot off our mouths" and get in all kinds of trouble. Then, realizing our foolishness, we run *from* God instead of *to* Him.

I cannot imagine what Peter must have felt when they arrested and crucified Jesus. Jesus had taken Peter under His wing, and Peter repaid Him by swearing he didn't know Him and wasn't with Him. Surely Peter must have been heavy laden with grief at that moment.

Jesus was more than just Peter's Teacher and Master. He was his Friend. Jesus said that He called His disciples *"My friends"* when they did what He commanded them. The near disasters at sea, the feeding of the multitudes, the sick healed and the dead raised (including his own mother-in-law) ... all these miracles must have haunted Peter around the clock. "He was the Son of God," Peter surely reminded himself, and "I betrayed Him. Now He's gone. How I wish I could have told Him I was sorry." Hour after painful hour passed for Peter, each seeming to last days. When a man or woman is in the grip of despair, the pain only intensifies with the passing of time.

It is at this point that a decision is made to either be a victim or be a victor. When grief, pain and sorrow have seized our thoughts and penetrated our souls, we desperately want to run and hide. We curse, accuse, blame and rationalize ... anything to take away the pain. In the process, God often becomes the victim. Our heavenly Father is the recipient of our anger, because we expect Him to deliver us BEFORE the trial comes. But He doesn't work that way. *Life* doesn't work that way.

James taught that we are to *"count it all joy"* when we encounter trials, *"knowing,"* he said, that the testing of our faith brings perseverance. Perseverance is that character trait that enables us not to give up when everything around us is screaming "Surrender!" Did Peter have it? He did. How do I know? Because he had at least one other opportunity to walk away from Jesus, and he didn't do it.

Peter as Disciple

> *And He said, "Therefore I have said to you that no one can come to Me unless it has been granted to him by My Father."*
> *From that time many of His disciples went back and walked with Him no more.*
> *Then Jesus said to the twelve, "Do you also want to go away?"*
> *But Simon Peter answered Him, "Lord, to whom shall we go? You have the words of eternal life. Also we have come to believe and know that You are the Christ, the Son of the living God."*   John 6:65-69 (NKJ)

"Where would I go?" Peter asked. He was given the opportunity to run and didn't. Why? Peter had made a commitment, and he was determined to follow through with it. It would certainly have been tempting for him to go back to what he knew. Fishing for natural fish was easier than fishing for men. But Peter had seen too much and gone too far to turn back now.

There was something about being with Jesus that

was like no other experience on Earth. Seeing His compassion, beholding His miracle touch, hearing His timeless words of wisdom — all live and in person. The gentle way He spoke to the downtrodden, the inimitable fashion in which He put the Pharisees in their place ... Peter was an eyewitness in every one of these instances.

But Peter was still Peter, and often He would say something profound followed immediately by something stupid. Small wonder Peter was unsure about his place in the Kingdom after Jesus died! Yet there was something different about this man, something that separated him from Judas, the other disciple who betrayed Jesus. I believe it was perseverance. Peter was, after all, a fisherman!

Anyone who's ever fished more than a few times knows that you don't always catch your limit in the first five minutes. I recall going fishing with my Mom and Dad when we were all still at home. What an experience! Dad tried to teach us how to fish, but some of us didn't catch on very well (no pun intended). Of course, patience (i.e., perseverance) had a lot to do with it. Dad liked to fish so much that he would try for hours before giving up. I reasoned later that he must have applied this same principle to his children, for we were all tough to raise sometimes. Yet he stuck with it.

Mom was always the one who dealt with the

messy end of fishing. She would remove the head and scales from the fish, then wash them in the sink. Afterwards, she'd roll them in an egg-and-flour mix and fry them in butter. Boy, did those fish taste great!

We had mostly pan fish in our area, with an occasional trout to eat after we moved to Montana. Anyway, it often seemed like the story "The Little Red Hen." At least that's what Mom kept reminding us of. She would do all the work, and we'd show up in time to eat. Personally, I thought it was a sweet deal!

The point is fishing isn't for cowards. It's a long way from casting to the fish fry, so hang on. It's messy and frustrating, but sometimes it's even fun. Perhaps Peter knew this, and that's why he never gave up. Jesus told Peter that he would be changed from a fisherman to a fisher of men. That takes even more time.

Peter as Victor

On the evening of that first day of the week, when the disciples were together, with the doors locked for fear of the Jews, Jesus came and stood among them and said, "Peace be with you!" Afterward Jesus appeared again to his disciples, by the Sea of Tiberias. It happened this way: Simon Peter, Thomas (called Didymus),

*Nathanael from Cana in Galilee, the sons of
Zebedee, and two other disciples were together.
"I'm going out to fish," Simon Peter told them,
and they said, "We'll go with you." So they
went out and got into the boat, but that night
they caught nothing.*

John 20:19 and 21:1-3 (NIV)

At this point, Peter had seen the empty tomb. In
verse 22, Jesus appeared to the disciples in the Upper Room, breathed on them, and gave them the
Holy Spirit. A few verses later, Peter was back fishing. As some of the gang at work would say, "What's
up with that?"

This is our greatest mistake on the road to victory
following a setback. We *go back* to what we know.
I've seen it happen so many times. People get hurt,
badly sometimes. They launched out into uncharted
waters, whereupon their ship sank, and they nearly
drowned. "No more sailing for me!" they cry.

But our Father didn't call us to the safety of the
seashore. He called us to go. That means risk, and
I've discovered that if you want God's best for you
(and for His Kingdom), you have to get wet at some
point.

There are no shortcuts to our destiny (destination).
Peter, I believe, knew that. Whether in the Upper
Room or on a boat, he was deep in thought. He
didn't want to let Jesus down ever! Yet he had.

Later, Jesus told the disciples to wait for the Holy Spirit. This time, Peter was obedient, and stayed in the Upper Room as Jesus had instructed. This would lead to a powerful transformation, after which Peter was never the same again:

> *Now Peter and John went up together to the temple at the hour of prayer, the ninth hour. And a certain man lame from his mother's womb was carried, whom they laid daily at the gate of the temple which is called Beautiful, to ask alms from those who entered the temple; who, seeing Peter and John about to go into the temple, asked for alms. And fixing his eyes on him, with John, Peter said, "Look at us." So he gave them his attention, expecting to receive something from them. Then Peter said, "Silver and gold I do not have, but what I do have I give you: In the name of Jesus Christ of Nazareth, rise up and walk." And he took him by the right hand and lifted him up, and immediately his feet and ankle bones received strength. So he, leaping up, stood and walked and entered the temple with them— walking, leaping, and praising God.* Acts 3:1-8 (NKJ)

What a stark contrast this is to the Peter we came to know in the four gospels. The fearful, split-personality, up-one-minute-and-down-the-next guy is gone, replaced by a power-filled servant of the Most High God. Simon "The Flake" has disappeared, and in his place is Peter, "The Rock" that Jesus said he would be.

The Scriptures are filled with examples of lives transformed by the power of God in order to accomplish His divine purpose. Oftentimes, the men and women in question were ordinary people, at least by our standards. They were defeated and broken many times, but God *"who is rich in mercy"* stuck with them, brought them through to victory, and then used them for His glory.

But it took two things on the part of the people being transformed: trust and obedience. When our Father tells us to do and to be, He will provide all we need to get the job done. Focusing on a failed relationship, corrupt leadership or any other "ship" will only lead to more destruction. Just get back on the ship and get under way.

We will never become victors if we behave like victims. Peter knew this, and that is why he became the ultimate victor.   ✷

Part IV

Victim ... or Victor

Outside were conflicts, inside were fears. Nevertheless God ...

Who shall separate us from the love of Christ? Shall tribulation, or distress, or persecution, or famine, or nakedness, or peril, or sword? As it is written: "For Your sake we are killed all day long; we are accounted as sheep for the slaughter." Yet in all these things we are more than conquerors through Him who loved us.

Paul

Chapter 8

Victim or Victor: Which Am I?

As I was writing this book, it seemed to me that recalling even a small portion of it would be difficult for most readers. When I finished the section entitled "The Victim Mentality," God showed me an outline — a checklist if you will — that can show us when we're living and acting like victims. At the end of the next section, He did the same, contrasting this with living and acting like the victors that God created us to be.

Please read through each of the points slowly and pray that our heavenly Father will show you where you may need to change.

Victims: The Telltale Signs

1. Absent real peace, victims are caught up in anger, leading in some cases to violence. A distorted sense of justice plagues such persons, making them angry and bitter toward everyone, especially their oppressors (both real and imagined).

2. They are unable to function effectively in relationships because they "need" someone to rescue them from the pain they feel. Victims are typically users when dealing with others because they are incapable (at that point in their lives) of giving. Therefore, they are usually involved in destructive relationships.

3. They also avoid relationships altogether. Victims are caught up in the past, and thus have "frozen" their future. Fear has taken over, keeping them from receiving love. These people usually have a long and sometimes distorted memory regarding the numerous offenses that are holding them back.

4. They are always giving their resumes, even in casual situations. This stems from a lack of self-worth. Victims believe nothing good will

happen to them because everyone is against them. Therefore, they feel it necessary to build themselves up in the eyes of others.

5. The smiles on the faces and the laughter in the voices of victims are cover-ups for the intense pain they feel. Instead of expressing the joy of the Lord, victims hide their hurt behind the illusion of happiness. Giving their resumes shows that they need others to think they "have it all together."

6. Victims have no joy at all, and they are constantly complaining. Need I say more?

7. Victims are defeated in thought, word and deed, in good times and bad, at home, at work at everything — even in victory.

Victors: The Indisputable Evidence

1. Victors are epitomized by the word *peaceful*.
    When they become angry, it is a righteous an-
    ger, resulting in a godly response. They never
    demand justice, but always plead for mercy.
    The command to love your enemies and pray
    for your oppressors is their top priority.

2. Victors function effectively in relationships be-
    cause, like Jesus, they are easily touched by the
    pain others feel. Victors are always givers when
    dealing with others because they are empow-
    ered to heal the brokenhearted. Compassion is
    their lifestyle.

3. Victors develop relationships with men and
    women from all walks of life. They have bur-
    ied the past, realizing they have been crucified
    and risen with Christ. The future is bright be-
    cause fear has been conquered, and thus love
    is made perfect in them. As God continually
    does for them, these men and women forgive
    the numerous offenses heaped upon them each
    day. They view Christ's commands as black
    and white, but never the conduct of others.

4. Victors never try to impress people or put others in their place. They believe good will happen to them because God is for them. Therefore, they have no need to build themselves up in the eyes of others, or to tear others down in order to build themselves up in their own eyes. Secure in their divine call and purpose, they *"press [forward] toward the mark."*

5. The smiles on the faces and the laughter in the voices of victors are real. The joy of the Lord is their strength. Because they focus on His promises instead of on their pain and persecution, others see their joy and are drawn to them and to the One they serve. The Father is proud of them.

6. Victors are always rejoicing and constant in praise. Need I say more?

7. Victors are victorious in thought, word and deed, in good times and bad, at home, at work, at everything — even in defeat.

God bless, and Godspeed to you all!

✳

Come to Me, all you who labor and are heavy laden, and I will give you rest. Take My yoke upon you and learn from Me, for I am gentle and lowly in heart, and you will find rest for your souls.

Jesus, NKJ